The Challenge of Subtitling Offensive and Taboo Language into Spanish

Full details of all our other publications can be found on http://www.multilingual-matters.com, or by writing to Multilingual Matters, St Nicholas House, 31-34 High Street, Bristol, BS1 2AW, UK.

The Challenge of Subtitling Offensive and Taboo Language into Spanish

A Theoretical and Practical Guide

José Javier Ávila-Cabrera

MULTILINGUAL MATTERS
Bristol • Jackson

DOI https://doi.org/10.21832/AVILA4860
Library of Congress Cataloging in Publication Data
A catalog record for this book is available from the Library of Congress.
Names: Ávila-Cabrera, José Javier, author.
Title: The Challenge of Subtitling Offensive and Taboo Language into Spanish:
   A Theoretical and Practical Guide/José Javier Ávila-Cabrera.
Description: Bristol; Jackson: Multilingual Matters, [2023] | Includes bibliographical
   references, filmography, and index. | Summary: "This book presents a clear and
   concise guide to understanding the concepts of offensive and taboo language and
   how this type of language can be subtitled into Spanish for Spain. It includes
   an array of examples from recent films and TV series as well as exercises which
   allow the reader to put theory into practice"—Provided by publisher.
Identifiers: LCCN 2022039502 (print) | LCCN 2022039503 (ebook) |
   ISBN 9781800414860 (hardback) | ISBN 9781800414884 (epub) |
   ISBN 9781800414877 (pdf)
Subjects: LCSH: Subtitles (Motion pictures, television, etc.)—Spain. |
   Taboo, Linguistic.
Classification: LCC P306.93 .A95 2023 (print) | LCC P306.93 (ebook) |
   DDC 468/.02—dc23/eng/20221018
LC record available at https://lccn.loc.gov/2022039502
LC ebook record available at https://lccn.loc.gov/2022039503

British Library Cataloguing in Publication Data
A catalogue entry for this book is available from the British Library.

ISBN-13: 978-1-80041-486-0 (hbk)
ISBN-13: 978-1-83668-130-4 (pbk)

Multilingual Matters
UK: St Nicholas House, 31-34 High Street, Bristol, BS1 2AW, UK.
USA: Ingram, Jackson, TN, USA.
Authorised Representative: Easy Access System Europe – Mustamäe tee 50, 10621
Tallinn, Estonia gpsr.requests@easproject.com.

Website: www.multilingual-matters.com
Bluesky: https://bsky.app/profile/multi-ling-mat.bsky.social
Twitter: Multi_Ling_Mat
Facebook: https://www.facebook.com/multilingualmatters
Blog: www.channelviewpublications.wordpress.com

Copyright © 2023 José Javier Ávila-Cabrera.

All rights reserved. No part of this work may be reproduced in any form or by any means without permission in writing from the publisher.

The policy of Multilingual Matters/Channel View Publications is to use papers that are natural, renewable and recyclable products, made from wood grown in sustainable forests. In the manufacturing process of our books, and to further support our policy, preference is given to printers that have FSC and PEFC Chain of Custody certification. The FSC and/or PEFC logos will appear on those books where full certification has been granted to the printer concerned.

Typeset by Deanta Global Publishing Services, Chennai, India.

To Joy

Contents

Illustrations	ix
Acknowledgements	xi
Abbreviations	xiii

1	Introduction	1
2	Audiovisual Translation	4
	2.1 Subtitling	6
	2.1.1 Types of subtitles	8
	2.1.1.1 Intralingual subtitles	8
	2.1.1.2 Interlingual subtitles	13
	2.1.1.3 Bilingual subtitles	14
	2.1.1.4 Multilingual subtitles	14
	2.1.1.5 Types of subtitles in foreign language learning	14
	2.2 Subtitling Conventions	15
	2.2.1 Technical constraints	15
	2.2.2 Subtitle synchronisation	17
	2.2.3 Formal appearance of subtitles	18
	2.2.4 Text reduction	19
	2.3 Punctuation and Orthotypography	20
	2.4 The Semiotic Dimension of Subtitling	21
	2.5 Subtitled Products	22
	2.6 Manipulation	24
	2.6.1 Patronage	25
	2.6.2 Ideological manipulation	26
	2.6.3 Censorship	27
	2.6.3.1 Why does censorship take place?	28
	2.6.3.2 Types of censorship	29
	2.6.3.3 Censorship in the US	31
	2.6.3.4 Censorship in the UK	33
	2.6.3.5 Censorship in Spain	34
	2.7 Exercises	38

3	Offensive and Taboo Language	43
	3.1 Historical Approach	43
	3.2 Terminological Concepts	44
	3.3 Taxonomy of Offensive and Taboo Terms	46
	3.4 Modulating the Language Style: Euphemism, Orthophemism and Dysphemism	49
	3.5 An Approach to (Im)Politeness	52
	3.6 The Impact and Treatment of Offensive and Taboo Language	54
	3.6.1 A cultural approach	54
	3.6.2 An approach based on audiovisual translation	55
	3.6.3 Proposals for subtitling offensive and taboo language	57
	3.7 Research on Offensive and Taboo Areas	58
	3.7.1 Research on offensive and taboo topics	59
	3.7.2 Offensive and taboo language in subtitling	60
	3.8 Exercises	64
4	Model of Analysis for Offensive/Taboo Language	72
	4.1 Method, Translation Strategies vs Translation Techniques	72
	4.1.1 Subtitling strategies	73
	4.1.2 Subtitling techniques	78
	4.1.2.1 Transfer of the load	79
	4.1.2.2 Non-transfer of the load	80
	4.2 Research Design	81
	4.2.1 Purpose(s)	82
	4.2.2 Conceptual framework	83
	4.2.3 Research questions	85
	4.2.4 Methods	86
	4.2.5 Sampling procedures	87
	4.3 Exercises	87

Answer Key	99
References	142
Filmography	150
TV Series	152
Web Addresses	153
Index	154

Illustrations

Figures

Figure 2.1	Snapshot of *Snatch*	12
Figure 2.2	Example of a pyramidal layout	19
Figure 4.1	Example of conceptual framework	83
Figure 4.2	Example of manipulation in film subtitles for flight versions	84

Tables

Table 2.1	Example of correct and incorrect segmentation	18
Table 2.2	Example of language combinations in *See* by Apple TV	23
Table 3.1	Taxonomy of offensive and taboo language	47
Table 3.2	Examples of dysphemism, orthophemism and euphemism	51
Table 4.1	Taxonomy of subtitling techniques for the transfer of offensive and taboo language	78

Acknowledgements

I would like express my deepest gratitude to Dr Noa Talaván and Professor Jorge Díaz Cintas for all they have taught me throughout my university career. They have been a great source of inspiration to me; to my friends and colleagues Dr Avelino Corral Esteban and Dr Pilar Rodríguez-Arancón, for their indefatigable encouragement; to Professor Roberto A. Valdeón for his interest in my research studies, which is mutual; to Dr Antonio Roales Ruiz, for all I learnt from him about the field of professional subtitling when working together, and for all his helpful comments on the technicalities of subtitling. I would also like to thank other colleagues for their help through various consultations about censorship in Spain such as Dr María Pérez L. de Heredia, Dr Cristina Gómez Castro, Dr Camino Gutiérrez Lanza, Dr Rosa Rabadán and Dr Sergio Lobejón Santos.

My special thanks to audiovisual translators who have coped with the difficulties inherent in the subtitling of offensive and taboo language. Thanks to all their contributions to the audiovisual translation industry – this book has assembled a number of their subtitles into Spanish – and which through their descriptive analysis will inspire undergraduates and future subtitlers, hopefully in the same way they have motivated me to look into the subtleties of this type of language which has received little attention from academia over many years.

I am also very grateful to all researchers from different areas who have broken taboos of their own in this field of research. These authors have greatly influenced my desire to explore taboo content in all its forms in audiovisual translation. I would also like to thank the reviewer of this book for all the insightful comments and suggestions made to improve it during the revision stage.

To my parents for having taught me the importance of love, respect and hard work, and especially to my mum for all her strength in dealing with adversity in life – something she has instilled in me.

Last but not least, this book is dedicated to my lovely wife Joy, an avid reader of all my work. Her support and encouragement while writing this book has been exceptional.

Abbreviations

AD   Audio Description
ATRAE   *Asociación de Traducción y Adaptación Audiovisual de España* [Association of Audiovisual Translation and Adaptation of Spain]
AVT   Audiovisual translation
BBC   British Broadcasting Corporation
CESyA   *Centro Español de Subtitulado y Audiodescripción* [Spanish Centre of Subtitling and Audio Description]
DTS   Descriptive translation studies
DTT   Digital terrestrial television
DVD   Digital video disc
L1   First language
L2   Second language
MPAA   Motion Picture Association of America
OTT   Over the top
RAE   *Real Academia Española* [Spanish Royal Academy]
SDH   Subtitling for the D/deaf or the hard of hearing
SL   Source language
SpS   *Subtítulos para sordos* [Subtitles for the deaf]
ST   Source text
TCR   Time code reader
TL   Target language
TS   Translation studies
TT   Target text
VCD   Video compact disc
VHS   Video home system
VOD   Video on demand

1 Introduction

Before I started conducting research almost a decade ago, I remember hearing people say 'these subtitles are very different from what the speakers say' or 'these subtitles do not translate what the speakers say', and this is a general thought of people not familiar with audiovisual translation (AVT). However, once you know the conventions of subtitling, you realise that subtitles are not a literal translation of the source text (ST) to the target text (TT), but a rendering of the linguistic, cultural and paralinguistic information on the screen. Simply put, it is the transfer of the gist we can hear and see on the screen given the technical constraints of this AVT mode.

I spent my university years as an undergraduate in Madrid watching films subtitled into Spanish in the very few cinemas that presented films in their original language. My interest in the way subtitlers rendered swear words and phrases into Spanish started just after meeting my PhD supervisors, Dr Noa Talaván and Professor Jorge Díaz Cintas. This interest turned into a passion for gaining some insights into the way offensive, taboo or vulgar language, as some authors define it, was subtitled into Spanish in Spain. This passion led me to conduct my own thorough research in this field. This book is a result of the research I have been conducting for the past several years. A brief description of its content is presented as follows.

Chapter 1 describes the contents of the book and its overall purpose, which is to provide readers (whether undergraduates, researchers or AVT professionals) with a clear and concise guide to understanding the concepts of what can be considered linguistically offensive (terms used with the aim of vilifying) and taboo (terms more or less welcome depending on the context in which they are uttered, the addressee, cultural background, etc.) (Ávila-Cabrera, 2014). There is a focus on how this type of language can be transferred via subtitles into Spanish (spoken in Spain). In addition to the technical and spatiotemporal restrictions of this AVT mode (Díaz Cintas, 2001a), there are other restrictions in the form of (self)censorship and (ideological) manipulation, which are also dealt with in this volume.

The scope of AVT in general is contextualised in Chapter 2. It then centres on subtitling as the AVT mode of interest here. A taxonomy of subtitles (Díaz Cintas & Remael, 2021) is presented along with other types of subtitles used in didactic subtitling (Talaván, 2012). Subtitling conventions are explored in order to provide the reader with an understanding of the technicalities and appearance of subtitles. Manipulation, an important element in AVT, is explained when approaching the concepts of patronage, ideological manipulation and censorship in all its forms, including the censorship exerted in the US, the UK and Spain. At the end of the chapter, 20 exercises are included which enable the theory on text reduction to be put into practice.

Chapter 3 is devoted to offensive and taboo language. The terminological concepts of the literature are revised along with different scholars' paradigms on this type of language. A taxonomy of offensive and taboo language (Ávila-Cabrera, 2014) is presented, re-elaborated and discussed, with special attention given to the impact this type of language can have in AVT. The way the tone of offensive and/or taboo language can be manipulated is explained through the concepts of euphemism, orthophemism and dysphemism (Allan & Burridge, 2006). The importance of the field of (im)politeness is also addressed. Some proposals when subtitling offensive and taboo language are developed with the aim of helping future subtitlers. The research literature in different scopes, as well as in AVT, is also discussed. There are 30 exercises based on the theoretical concepts developed in this section presented at the end of the chapter.

A model of analysis of offensive and taboo language is presented in Chapter 4. As translation operation tools, a discussion on translation strategies (Díaz Cintas & Remael, 2021) and techniques (Ávila-Cabrera, 2020) is developed with examples. In addition, a formula for how to create a research design (Robson, 2011) is illustrated on the basis of the purpose(s), conceptual framework, research questions, methods and sampling procedures based on the elements of interest in this book. Finally, 40 exercises based on the offensive/taboo category and subcategories, and translation strategies and techniques are provided at the end of the chapter.

A chapter titled 'Answer Key' is provided and includes all the exercises (borrowed from the films and TV series analysed) with their corresponding answer keys in order to present the reader with examples of the original subtitles (provided by the corresponding subtitlers) available on current digital platforms or on the digital video disc (DVD). All these exercises are aimed at the reader in order to put theory into practice. Far from being critical of subtitles produced by professionals, the goal here is to make use of the theoretical instruments (in the form of what can be considered offensive and/or taboo when modulating these terms during their transfer to subtitles) with which to understand the treatment of this type of language and, specifically, how this language has been subtitled into Spanish for the Spanish audience.

This book combines theoretical and practical approaches with the purpose of providing insights into the practice of subtitling and aims to contribute to the literature on AVT and offensive and taboo language, a field which is still lacking a large body of theoretical-practical publications. If we consider the language combinations used (English into Spanish) in subtitling with the exercises included, this book can help readers put into practice the theoretical concepts addressed within. I hope this monograph is useful not only to undergraduates and researchers, but also to future audiovisual translators seeking to acquire further knowledge into the transfer of offensive and taboo language in subtitling.

2 Audiovisual Translation

We are living in a technological world where electronic devices allow us instant access to information and audiovisual content. A few decades ago, we could not imagine how easy it would be today to use social networks to be in touch with our contacts, to be able to read the news on a laptop, tablet or mobile phone, and how convenient it would be for us to watch our favourite TV show or film from home or via mobile technology on the go.

The need to make foreign audiovisual content available to speakers who are not yet proficient in a foreign language or to allow viewers to understand linguistic variations, dialects, slang, etc., has led to AVT becoming a professional practice of paramount importance in the distribution of this content. In the last decade, we have witnessed a new audiovisual market thanks to streaming platforms. An example of this can be seen in the boom of platforms, such as Netflix, Prime Video, HBO, Apple TV and Disney+, which are dominating the international market and are quickly becoming a dominant force in Spain. The cinema may become endangered due to the production of many films and TV series by these platforms, considering that the price of a cinema ticket can pay for a monthly subscription to a streaming platform. The vast amount of audiovisual content that is available online, coupled with the linguistic combinations of dubbing and subtitling, for instance, requires the hiring of more and more audiovisual translators. These translators are also gaining more visibility as they are now mentioned in the closing credits, whereas a decade ago, credit was only usually given to the subtitler.

Díaz Cintas and Remael (2021) described the professional practice of AVT when the cinema was invented between the end of the 19th century and the beginning of the 20th century. However, AVT was ignored in academic circles until the mid-1990s thanks to the propagation and dissemination of audiovisual content. As a subfield within translation studies (TS), AVT deals with the transfer of multimedia and multimodal text into another language or into the same language and culture. The terminology used in this audiovisual field in the past few decades has been diverse, as enumerated by Orero (2004): film dubbing (Fodor, 1976), *traducción subordinada* or constrained translation (Mayoral *et al.*, 1988; Titford, 1982), film translation (Snell-Hornby, 1988), film and TV translation (Delabastita, 1989), screen translation (Mason, 1989), media translation (Eguíluz *et al.*, 1994), film communication (Lecuona Lerchundi, 1994), *traducción fílmica* or film translation (Díaz Cintas, 1997), (multi)media translation (Gambier & Gottlieb, 2001) and AVT (Baker & Hochel, 1998; Díaz Cintas & Remael, 2021; Luyken *et al.*, 1991; Shuttleworth & Cowie, 1997). Today, the acronym AVT is most commonly used because it encompasses all modes of translation for production or postproduction in any media or format.

It is well known that AVT concerns any type of text such as those of films, TV series, documentaries, cartoons and video games, and also several media such us TV, cinema, the internet and streaming platforms. AVT encompasses diverse traditional modes, namely subtitling, dubbing, voiceover, narration, AD and simultaneous/consecutive interpreting (Díaz Cintas & Anderman, 2009).

Díaz Cintas and Remael (2021) also mentioned emerging translation modes in terms of media accessibility, that is, subtitling for the D/deaf or hard of hearing (SDH),[1] which can be interlingual and intralingual; audio description for the blind and the partially sighted (AD), which can also be combined with audio subtitling (AST); rewriting (subtitling or SDH) and surtitling, 'the translation, across languages, or transcription, within the same idiom, of dialogue and lyrics in live events such as operas, musical shows, concerts, conferences and theatre performances' (Díaz Cintas & Remael, 2021: 9–10); and revoicing (dubbing, voiceover, narration, AD and interpreting). Live subtitling concerns the *ad hoc* production of subtitles for live programmes.

Other emerging practices are 'fansubs', 'fandubs' (subtitling and dubbing carried out by fans), 'webtoons' (animated comic strips created by amateurs) and 'scanlations' (uploaded scanned translations). Díaz Cintas (2018) established a taxonomy of these practices, such as 'cybertitles', divided into 'fansubs', 'guerrilla subtitles' and 'altruistic subtitles'. They can also be divided into 'genuine subtitles' and 'fakesubs'. In addition, Chaume (2018) described 'fundubs' (dubbing aimed at making parody through creative translation), usually homemade TV series, cartoons or trailers, which have not yet been broadcast in the target culture or language. These practices also have the name 'gag dubbing'. 'Funads' are comedic audio descriptions that are intended to replace the original audio for a new creative one. An app that is currently very popular on WhatsApp messages is MadLipz. Users can dub a video included in the app just for fun.

Current society is dominated by the use of information technology (IT) and audiovisual media. These have become common vehicles in the fields of communication, information, culture and leisure, and AVT has gained a prime role on a global basis. Although all the aforementioned translation modes share some features, they cannot be grouped and studied as a single entity; instead, they must be approached in different ways because they operate under certain and specific conditions.

In the case of subtitling, new layouts are also being used, as is the case with creative subtitles. Chaume (2018) explained that they can appear in different forms (capital or lower case), italics, in different positions on the screen (as with multilingual subtitles) and even with unusual fonts and colours.

Apart from the difficulties faced by audiovisual translators in terms of the linguistic transfer of the source language (SL) into the target language (TL), there are other paramount difficulties to consider in AVT (not approached in this book) which entail further challenges to the translation process such as the treatment of humour (Chiaro, 2018; Martínez Sierra, 2006; Zabalbeascoa, 2005), how to translate puns (Delabastita, 2014), discourse markers in AVT (Chaume, 2004a), gay subjects and identity (Martínez Pleguezuelos, 2021; Ranzato, 2012), cultural references and intercultural mediation (Guillot, 2020; Pedersen, 2015), linguistic variation (Bolaños García Escribano, 2017; Díaz Cintas & Remael, 2021), intertextuality (Bogucki, 2020; Botella Tejera, 2018), accessible filmmaking (Romero-Fresco, 2019), eye-tracking studies in subtitling (Szarkowska & Bogucka, 2019), multilingual films (Díaz Cintas, 2011; de Higes-Andino, 2014; Tamayo Masero & Manterola Agirrezabalaga, 2019), multilingualism and humour (Dore, 2019; Zabalbeascoa, 2020) and humour and animated films (Gonzalez Vera, 2015). Scholars specialise in different fields and their contributions can be of great assistance to translators in general, and audiovisual translators in particular.

2.1 Subtitling

Díaz Cintas (2009) highlighted that subtitling is one of the foremost modes of AVT, and today it is a very well positioned field thanks to a flurry of activity, such as multiple research publications, conferences at the international level, the development of university and professional courses, and the writing of academic theses. Most audiovisual content users are familiar with AVT modes, although they might not understand the intrinsic conventions of each of them. It has been a long time since the first book on subtitling was published (Ivarsson & Carroll, 1998), which introduced a code of good subtitling practice, and even though the market has evolved significantly, many of these conventions are still valid.

Subtitling is the presentation of a written text on the screen in synchrony with the original verbal or written message shown. Among many possible definitions, Díaz Cintas and Remael (2021) defined interlingual subtitling as

> a translation practice that consists in presenting a written text, generally on the lower part of the screen, that aims to recount the original dialogue

exchanged among the various speakers, as well as the other verbal information that is transmitted visually (letters, inserts, graffiti, text messages, inscriptions, placards, and the like), and aurally (songs, voices off, voiceover narration). (Díaz Cintas & Remael, 2021: 9)

If we pay attention to the process of subtitling, we can see the complexity of this practice in which various professionals take part, as explained by Díaz Cintas (2008). In the first instance, the primary client (the production or distribution company and/or TV station) contracts the subtitling company. The programme is then watched to verify that the copy provided by the client is not damaged and that the dialogue list (if provided) is correct and contains all the information (signs, inserts, songs and the like) to be translated. A working copy of the original is then made, usually with anti-pirate inserts, and is sent to the translator who, when not working with templates, is also responsible for spotting the programme, which, in the professional and educational jargon, is also known as cueing, timing or originating. At this stage, the dialogue is divided into units to be subtitled and the 'in' and 'out' cues of the subtitle are indicated, that is, the subtitle must appear on the screen when the words are uttered or can be read from the screen until they are said or are visible on the screen. The subtitles are spotted by using a time code reader (TCR), which professional subtitle editors use to indicate the hours:minutes:seconds:frames, while non-professional editors use milliseconds instead of frames (Ávila-Cabrera, 2014). Before translating the script, it is recommended to watch the film in its entirety so that notes can be taken on problematic issues. Once the translation is finished, it is sent to the subtitling company, where it will be revised and proofread. A simulation of the subtitles will be carried out with the client, and if it is satisfactory to the client, the next stage takes place. The subtitles are laser-engraved on the celluloid, covering the film with a black dust, which is why the celluloid is washed and dried. A final viewing will take place in order to check that the engraving and washing of the subtitles are good enough before the programme is submitted to the client, ready for its screening.

Three professionals are involved in the subtitling process. First, the spotter, who is the person in charge of deciding the 'in' and 'out' cues of the subtitles and producing templates and master titles in which useful information for the translation task is usually incorporated. This part is paramount since subtitles that are not properly spotted can ruin the viewing of the audiovisual programme regardless of its linguistic quality, considering that the subtitles would not match what is on the screen simultaneously. Second, the translator, who is responsible for the linguistic transfer of the SL into the TL. In intralingual subtitling, we refer to the transfer from a ST into a TT. Obviously, at this stage, the translator's wit and linguistic quality are at play. Third, and less frequently, the adaptor, who is an expert in the challenges this media poses, oversees the condensation and reduction of the TT, working on the translation provided by the translator. Nowadays, it is very common that the same person is in charge of the spotting, linguistic transfer and adaptation.

The subtitling industry has evolved significantly in recent years. To address these changes, the following sections discuss the most recent standards present in this AVT mode.

2.1.1 Types of subtitles

Before addressing the most common types of subtitles, we need to travel back in time and refer to intertitles as the precursors of subtitles, 'also known as "title cards" and can be defined as a piece of filmed, printed text that appears between scenes' (Díaz Cintas & Remael, 2007: 26). They were most commonly used in silent films and appeared as short sentences written in white on a black background so that spectators could follow the plot. Their main goal was to transmit dialogue exchanges and descriptive narrative material in tandem with the images on screen. When soundtrack arrived, these intertitles all but disappeared. Occasionally, they appear in contemporary films, as in *The Artist* (Michel Hazanavicius, 2011), and are generally known as 'inserts'.

From a linguistic point of view, Díaz Cintas and Remael (2021: 11) distinguished between intralingual (which include subtitles for karaoke and singing alone; for dialects, accents and poor quality recordings; and Asian subtitles called Telop, Tù cáo [-吐槽] and Dànmù [-弹幕]) and interlingual subtitles (monolingual, bilingual and multilingual). Both types can be used for (foreign) language learning, and are aimed at hearers and people who are D/deaf or hard of hearing. The various types of subtitles are examined from a linguistic point of view in the following sections. The Asian subtitles Telop, Tù cáo [-吐槽] and Dànmù [-弹幕], which are less popular in Europe, will be described in the following section.

2.1.1.1 Intralingual subtitles

Intralingual subtitling, also known as 'same-language subtitling' (SLS) (Díaz Cintas & Remael, 2021: 12), entails a change from oral to written language, but the subtitles themselves are in the same language as the dialogue. This is a form of audiovisual communication that is particularly common nowadays thanks to the technological and educational developments of the 21st century, and society's greater awareness of the needs of people with sensory impairments. Luyken *et al.* (1991) stated that intralingual subtitling is commonly used in domestic programmes for viewers with hearing impairment, that is, subtitling for people who are D/deaf or hard of hearing (Díaz Cintas & Remael, 2021). However, today intralingual subtitles are also highly consumed by language learners or users who just want to improve their listening skills, that is, they are used by users who are hearers or D/deaf or hard of hearing.

According to Neves (2009), intralingual subtitles are primarily addressed to people who are D/deaf or hearing impaired to allow accessibility to audiovisual media. In the US, these subtitles are known as captions or inserts, and they can also refer to written text superimposed on the original picture. Parks (1994) distinguished between open subtitles/captions and closed captions; while the former are engraved on the film (open), the latter are hidden (closed) and must be activated by the viewer. Nowadays with diverse audiovisual products, the abbreviation [CC] can be seen, which corresponds to closed captions (Talaván *et al.*, 2016), which are common on YouTube videos and streaming platforms for instance.

More recent smart TVs provide users with remote controls with a subtitle button. However, during the analogue period, users could view subtitles through teletext on television in most European countries. These subtitles were traditionally activated through an independent signal, using 'page 888 in the UK or on page 888 in most of Spain' (Neves, 2005: 112).

In SDH, the actors' dialogue can be displayed in subtitles of three or even four lines, and one of its unique features, which differentiates it from other types, is that SDH displays not only the dialogue exchanges, but also paralinguistic information that is important for understanding the storyline such as irony, laughter, cries, a knock on the door and background sounds (Díaz Cintas & Remael, 2021). There are numerous ways of dealing with visual and audio information. Sometimes, the subtitle colour changes, indicating to the viewers that a different character is speaking or the subtitles themselves can be repositioned to appear right below the speaker. However, as Díaz Cintas and Remael (2021: 12) stated, 'over the top (OTT) operators prefer to use labels to identify the speakers'.

SDH has made rapid strides in recent years thanks to the pressure of groups supporting the interests of this audience. Intralingual subtitles are most common in the UK and the US (Díaz Cintas & Anderman, 2009) and corporations like the BBC are positioned as some of the most advanced providers in this area. Since 2008, the BBC has been broadcasting 100% of its programmes with subtitles for the D/deaf or hard of hearing, and since May 2008, subtitles have been available on more than 90% of BBC iPlayer programmes for downloading or streaming. In 2018, the BBC published a guide to subtitling in English for any type of user willing to produce subtitles or open/closed captions. In addition, live subtitling has been a reality in the last decades, as discussed by Díaz Cintas and Remael (2021), due to the recent laws passed in many countries obliging television stations to broadcast accessible programmes with this service for example.

In the case of Spain, one of the groups promoting audiovisual accessibility through SDH and AD is CESyA (*Centro Español de Subtitulado y Audiodescripción*) [Spanish Centre of Subtitling and Audio Description] (Orero et al., 2007), which was created at the end of 2005. This centre not only deals with research and the dissemination of accessibility, but also offers services and education aimed at promoting audiovisual content in various formats, with the goal of making television accessible to all types of users.

Intralingual subtitles can also be used for language learning purposes, as a didactic tool with great educational potential for the learning and teaching of foreign languages, especially to people with limited knowledge of the language of the country in which they reside, such as immigrants and foreign language students.

The educational value of intralingual subtitles has certainly been appreciated by a number of companies in the past (Díaz Cintas & Remael, 2021). For example, Columbia Tristar Home Video commercialised the series *Speak Up* (1982), a collection of films in English subtitled into English, so that the viewers had the chance to follow the speech visually, paying attention to the words that they could not understand from the soundtrack. Another example of a learning-oriented product is a collection of classic cartoons with English subtitles called *Diviértete con el inglés* [Enjoy yourself with English], launched by the leading Spanish newspaper *El País* in 2002, in collaboration with Disney. These animation programmes were produced for young children to enable them to become acquainted with English.

The arrival of the DVD in the 1990s meant the consolidation of didactic subtitles, which are different from SDH. Some distributors such as Disney and Paramount have been commercialising films with two tracks of subtitles: one for D/deaf or hard of hearing and another in English for other users (Díaz Cintas & Remael, 2021). The latter are a good tool for children who are in the process of language acquisition, to improve their literacy skills in their own mother tongue as well as for foreign language learners. All in all, it cannot be denied that intralingual subtitles have a huge learning potential intended to help a wide range of viewers.

Abundant research has been conducted on how the use of subtitles (both intralingual and interlingual) can improve second language acquisition (Lambert et al., 1981) and vocabulary recognition and association (Borrás & Lafayette, 1994). Authors such as Talaván (2010, 2013) have argued that the production of subtitles as an active task can, among other benefits, enhance the oral comprehension skills of students. Funded research projects like Levis (Learning via Subtitling, http://levis.cti.gr) (Sokoli, 2006), ClipFlair (Foreign Language Learning through Interactive Revoicing & Captioning of Clips, http://clipflair.net) (Sokoli, 2018), PluriTAV (Multilingualism, Translation and Language Teaching, http://citrans.uv.es/pluritav/) (Martínez Sierra, 2021) and Tradilex

(Audiovisual Translation as a Didactic Resource in Foreign Language Education, https://tradit.uned.es/proyecto-tradilex) (Talaván & Lertola, 2022) have advanced on this route by developing activities in this area.

'Karaoke', 'sing alone' and 'sing-a-long' also make use of intralingual subtitles (Díaz Cintas & Remael, 2021). These subtitles are presented with songs or musical films so that the users can sing along while reading the lyrics on screen. As pointed out by Díaz Cintas and Remael (2021), *The Sound of Music* (Robert Wise, 1965) was a huge hit in London when it was re-released with karaoke subtitles and was advertised in a central London cinema as 'The classic film musical, now with subtitles so everyone can join in!' Other films that followed suit were *The Rocky Horror Picture Show* (Jim Sharman, 1975), *Abba Live in Concert* (Lasse Hallström, 1977) and the musical *Joseph and the Amazing Technicolor Dreamcoat* (Peter Plummer, 1972). More recent popular musicals are *Moulin Rouge* (Baz Luhrmann, 2001), *Les Miserables* (Tom Hooper, 2012) and *The Greatest Showman* (Michael Gracey, 2017).

Intralingual subtitles are also used in films and programmes where accents, dialects and a certain intonation may be hard to understand even for native speakers of the language, as may be the case with widely spoken languages such as English, French and Spanish (Díaz Cintas & Remael, 2021). An example of these intralingual subtitles can be seen in *Trainspotting* (Danny Boyle, 1996) where the main characters, who are working-class drug addicts, speak with a strong Scottish accent, swear a lot and make full use of slang. This film was distributed in the US with English subtitles so that the viewers would be able to understand the lexical variation, local accent and slang. Other examples are main characters who are working class, gangs and criminals and whose accents can be hard to understand by other English native or non-native speakers as in the case of director Guy Ritchie's *Lock, Stock and Two Smoking Barrels* (1998), *Snatch* (2000) and *Rock n' Rolla* (2008). Figure 2.1 shows a snapshot of *Snatch* with English subtitles, which reproduce what traveller character Mickey O'Neil, played by Brad Pitt, is saying, which is barely understandable.

More and more streaming platforms such as Netflix, Apple TV and HBO are providing films and TV series with audio in Spanish and subtitles in Spanish for Spain and Latin American Spanish, for example, or the opposite. A prime example of this is the Mexican film *Roma* (Alfonso Cuarón, 2018), whose treatment of the subtitles was quite controversial, as it was broadcast on Netflix in Spain with European Spanish, rather than with Latin American subtitles. The director found the treatment of the subtitles offensive and stated in the Spanish newspaper *El País*: 'It's provincial, ignorant and offensive to Spaniards themselves. One of the things I most enjoy is the color and texture of other accents. It's as if [the films of Spanish director Pedro] Almodóvar needed to be subtitled' (Morales *et al.*, 2019). Other academics of the Spanish language such as

Figure 2.1 Snapshot of *Snatch*

Javier Pérez and Pedro Álvarez de Miranda expressed their unhappiness regarding the use of these subtitles. In an interview with the BBC, Díaz Cintas (2019)[2] was asked why European Spanish subtitles were considered offensive. He replied:

> I think the colonial past that Spain has had and still has comes up behind some of the ideas that happened circulated in these couple of days. This parochial approach to different variants of the language of Spanish spoken by other people and it had to be the colonial power that decided to translate back into the Spanish of Spain. And I think that is what is the trouble there, that sort of manipulation of the text. (Díaz Cintas, 2019)

As can be inferred, both Cuarón and the aforementioned scholars agreed on how unwelcome these subtitles in Spanish were. Contrary to what was previously discussed regarding films with hard to understand English variation given the nature of the characters (Guy Ritchie, 1998, 2000, 2008), it could be said that the language spoken in *Roma* differs to a large extent from the language spoken in Guy Ritchie's films. This is the reason why this was a controversial issue. Later on, after *Roma* was available on the platform, Netflix removed the Spanish subtitles (for Spain) leaving only Latin American Spanish.

In addition to intralingual subtitles, Díaz Cintas and Remael (2021) also referred to those on monitors in underground stations or in other public places to announce events, advertise products and provide general information. These subtitles are sometimes displayed on screens without sound in order to avoid disturbing people, for instance in *Metro de Madrid* (Madrid's underground).

Finally, Díaz Cintas and Remael (2021) described some lesser-known types of subtitles. First, Telop, which are Japanese and other Asian multicoloured, highly visible and intralingual captions

(Sasamoto *et al.*, 2017). Their aim is to influence the audience's interpretation by making the affective values of programmes more straightforward. Second, Tù cáo [吐槽] are Chinese subtitles that differ from what can be considered a faithful rendering of the ST, and instead show the translator's feelings or comments. Third, Dànmù [弹幕] appear on the top of a video, with viewers' comments and reactions. They are very popular in China and Japan.

2.1.1.2 Interlingual subtitles

Interlingual subtitles involve the translation from a SL into a TL. Luyken *et al.* (1991: 31) referred to this category as 'diagonal subtitling', not only because there is a change from one language to another, but also because there is a shift in mode from oral to written language: '[i]nterlingual subtitling [...] is used for foreign language films. This type is diagonal since the subtitle crosses over from speech in the SL to writing in the TL, thus changing both mode and language'. Other scholars, such as Gottlieb (2010), agreed with this view and also considered this type of subtitling diagonal.

Interlingual subtitles can address hearing as well as D/deaf or hard-of-hearing viewers and they are usually monolingual. Historically, in some European countries with a steadfast tradition in dubbing such as Spain, France, Italy, Germany and Austria, the D/deaf or hard of hearing could only watch programmes that had been made in their SLs and contained intralingual subtitles into those languages. In this situation, it was rather difficult for these viewers to access foreign programmes, considering that they were usually dubbed and had no subtitles. These viewers could only watch foreign programmes with standard subtitles, which meant that they missed out on relevant information, inasmuch as the paralinguistic information was not included in these subtitles (Díaz Cintas & Remael, 2021).

Interlingual subtitling has expanded worldwide thanks to digital terrestrial television (DTT), satellite TV, video compact disc (VCD), DVD, Blu-ray, the internet – especially with video on demand (VOD) – and 3D. For example, in Germany, the UK and Italy, it was possible to buy DVDs with two sets of subtitles, one for hearing audiences and another produced specifically for the D/deaf or hard of hearing. In Spain, SDH subtitles could be found on many DVDs and Blu-ray discs. In countries such as Portugal, Greece and the Scandinavian nations (where interlingual subtitles are the norm), some DVDs were provided with interlingual SDH (Neves, 2009). Nowadays, thanks to the prolific number of VOD platforms, the linguistic combination offer is becoming more and more complete, providing users with interlingual and intralingual subtitles as well as SDH, thereby addressing the needs of viewers with hearing impairments.

2.1.1.3 Bilingual subtitles

The use of bilingual subtitles, a variety of interlingual subtitles, is not widespread and tends to be restricted to countries and communities where two languages are spoken and have official status. In the words of Ivarsson and Carroll (1998: 28), 'subtitling a film simultaneously in two languages has been standard practice for many years in countries such as Finland and Belgium'. Díaz Cintas and Remael (2021) stated that in the case of Finland, Swedish and Finnish are official languages, and in Belgium, subtitles in cinemas can be found in French and Flemish. Outside Europe, in countries such as Jordan and Israel, both Hebrew and Arabic subtitles appear concurrently at the bottom of the screen. Sometimes, four-line subtitles may also appear, although the tendency is to use two-line subtitles so as not to overload the screen with too much information.

Bilingual subtitles are also used at international film festivals, where some films display two sets of subtitles in different languages to attract a wider audience. One of the two subtitle tracks is English, as it is the most international language, and the other set corresponds to the language of the country where the festival is being held: French in Cannes (https://www.festival-cannes.com), German in Berlinale (https://www.berlinale.de), Italian in Biennale (https://www.labiennale.org/it) and Spanish in San Sebastián (https://www.sansebastianfestival.com). Díaz Cintas and Remael (2021) pinpointed that, in China, bilingual subtitles are presented in Chinese and English on major digital platforms as well as on TV stations. Indeed, we can observe a tendency in audiences' tastes regarding the types of subtitles used.

2.1.1.4 Multilingual subtitles

When three or more languages appear subtitled on screen at the same time, they can be categorised as multilingual subtitles (Díaz Cintas & Remael, 2021). In countries such as Malaysia where programmes were broadcast analogically, these open subtitles appeared in Chinese, Malay and English. However, with the current technological advances, viewers can choose the closed subtitles they want to activate, for which reason multilingual subtitles are no longer common.

2.1.1.5 Types of subtitles in foreign language learning

Research has been carried out into how both interlingual and intralingual subtitles can enhance second language acquisition, foster vocabulary recognition and association and improve written and oral comprehension skills (reading and listening) and the production of written and oral skills (writing and speaking). Talaván (2012) has conducted extensive research in the field of didactic AVT in a foreign language learning (FLL) setting. For the terminology of subtitles used in this field, Talaván (2012: 28-30) distinguishes the following:

- Subtitles for the D/deaf or hard of hearing, which in Spanish are called *Subtítulos para sordos* (SpS) (subtitles for the deaf). Both the linguistic and paralinguistic information is transferred from the ST, making use of colours and up to four-line subtitles. Originally, these subtitles were intralingual, but nowadays interlingual SDH are also very common.
- Bimodal subtitles. Both the audio and the subtitles are in the same language, from a first language/second language (L1/L2) to an L1/L2. In other words, they are intralingual. They are useful in terms of oral and written comprehension and vocabulary acquisition.
- Traditional or standard subtitles. The audio is in the L2 and the subtitles are in the L1, that is, they are interlingual. They are used to help the learner understand the content more easily, considering that they facilitate input comprehension.
- Reverse subtitles. The audio is in the L1 and the subtitles are in the L2. They are another combination of interlingual subtitles. They are a good tool for improving written production and vocabulary acquisition.

The study presented by Talaván (2020) is of interest because the author develops a thorough discussion of the possibilities subtitles can offer researchers and learners of foreign languages by combining the taxonomy shown above with intralingual and interlingual types, and with other recent types in the form of creative subtitling.

2.2 Subtitling Conventions

Subtitling entails a type of transfer of the ST into the TT that requires text reduction, synchronisation and use of syntactic and stylistic rules. In this section, we will briefly describe some of the most common conventions of subtitling.

2.2.1 Technical constraints

The appearance of subtitles on screen is determined by three main factors: the assumed reading speed of the audience, the time available and the lexical volume of the original dialogue, which usually entails text reduction. Thus, subtitling deals with a type of constraint in the form of spatiotemporal limitations in which there is room for enhancing the representation of different types of languages (Guillot, 2019).

Subtitlers not only have to deal with the rendering of a ST into a TT while carrying out the translation process, but they also have to bear in mind the aforementioned restrictions that impinge on the choices they can make. Temporal and spatial restrictions do not permit subtitlers to write as many characters per line as they might deem necessary. We must clarify here that when we refer to characters, we are including spaces, numbers and typographical signs. Temporal and spatial constraints therefore constitute parameters of paramount importance that need to be fully considered in order to ensure ease of reading of the subtitles (Díaz Cintas & Remael, 2021).

In this respect, subtitles can appear on screen for a minimum of one second and a maximum of six seconds (Brondeel, 1994; d'Ydewalle et al., 1987) and occupy one line (known as one-liners) or two lines (known as two-liners). Some companies apply the 'six-second rule', based on the fact that the average viewer is capable of comfortably reading and assimilating the information contained in a two-line subtitle (some 70 characters in total) in six seconds. As noted by Díaz Cintas and Remael (2007), the six-second rule is based on a mathematical calculation:

> [t]wo frames allow for a subtitle space. Given that the cinema illusion requires the projection of 24 frames per second (and 25 in television), this means that subtitlers can enjoy 12 subtitling spaces per second. In six seconds, then, the total will be 72, which becomes 74 in companies using 37-character lines. This calculation implies a rather low reading speed of some 140 to 150 words per minute or about 2.5 words per second. (Díaz Cintas & Remael, 2007: 96–97)

Roales Ruiz (2014) proposed the following settings when configuring subtitle editors for the production of subtitles: single line maximum length: 39 characters; optimal characters/second: 14; maximum characters/second: 16; minimum duration of the subtitle: 1000 milliseconds (one second); maximum duration of the subtitle: 6000 milliseconds (six seconds); minimum gap between subtitles: 250 milliseconds (1/4 second). The optimal number of characters in Spanish subtitles is 35 characters per line and 70 characters for two-liners (Roales Ruiz, 2018). If the average viewer is capable of reading that number of characters in six seconds without missing the visual information, it should be possible to calculate the amount of text that can be written in shorter subtitles. In addition, three elements determine the duration of the subtitle: the reading speed of the target audience; the density of the ST; and the time available for the subtitle to be visible (Talaván et al., 2016).

More recent approaches advocate for other measures. According to Díaz Cintas and Remael (2021), thanks to advances in digital media, proportional fonts have been added to subtitling programs. This means that the restriction on characters to 35, 39 or even 40 is no longer a golden rule, as long as the subtitle is placed in the safe area. The width of the letters used varies and it is the final pixel width that determines the number of characters to be used. However, it is not unusual for subtitling vendors to establish the number of characters per line: 37–39 characters for TV, cinema and DVD, which was the norm for years, but now VOD platforms are allowing up to 42 characters.

Nowadays, technological advances are permitting professionals to make use of professional web-based systems in subtitling (Bolaños-García-Escribano et al., 2021). Among these, the authors mention cloud-based platforms such as eCaption (ecaption.eu), OOONA (ooona.net) and SubtitleNext (subtitlenext.com). It is for this reason that subtitlers must be aware of the tools offered by the professional market to make ample use of the software programs available.

2.2.2 Subtitle synchronisation

One of the most challenging elements of subtitling, as discussed by Díaz Cintas and Remael (2021), which directly affects how a viewer perceives the validity of the subtitles, is temporal synchronisation. This practice is also known as spotting, cueing or timing (and refers to the pairing of the subtitle with the dialogue). Simply put, we are dealing with the time when the subtitle should appear on the screen as the dialogue is spoken (known as the cue-in time) and when it disappears (known as the cue-out time), both times being shown by the TCR. This timing can become more difficult when various characters are talking at the same time, in which case, the subtitler needs to choose which information is essential and which information can be condensed or even eliminated. Díaz Cintas and Remael stated that in some cases when it is not possible to further condense the subtitle, pre-synchrony is permitted. This means that the subtitle will appear a few frames before the dialogue takes place. Other authors such as Roales Ruiz (2017) stated that the optimal practice is for the subtitle to appear a quarter of a second after the utterance is said, so that the brain can assimilate the linguistic oral information along with the written text on the screen, that is, the subtitle. However, Roales Ruiz did not support pre-synchrony of the subtitle as this can spoil some scenes, particularly when a humoristic element is involved in the dialogue. Nonetheless, there is mutual agreement among authors about the use of post-synchrony when spatiotemporal restrictions require it.

Another important aspect to take into account is when there is a change of shot. Roales Ruiz (2018) stated that when this happens, the subtitle should disappear, considering that a change of shot is the division of two consecutive shots. If the subtitle were to appear in two different shots, the visual effect would be that of a different exchange, which could confuse the viewer. In this case, viewers might think that there is a new subtitle, forcing them to reread the same subtitle. There are exceptions to this rule when the change of shot cannot be considered, and the subtitle needs to appear in two or more shots. This is when the subtitle is shorter than one second, which is the minimum duration, or when there is a sequence shot. As for the interval between subtitles, based on Bravo (2004), Roales Ruiz recommended a quarter of a second or six frames.

As has been discussed, proper synchronisation of the subtitle with the dialogue is essential to ensure the viewer's comprehension and enjoyment.

2.2.3 Formal appearance of subtitles

As far as the formal appearance of subtitles is concerned, Roales Ruiz (2017) asserted that the preference in Spain is to use fonts without serif in the subtitles and usually in white (common in cinemas and digital platforms) or yellow. The fonts are preferably Arial, Helvetica and Times New Roman and their size varies, though font size 32 seems to be standard in the industry (Díaz Cintas & Remael, 2021). The usual position of the subtitle is centred at the bottom of the screen. A one-liner must occupy the bottom line of a two-liner so that they are analogous. Regarding colour, although as already mentioned it is usually white, new VOD platforms are reinventing themselves. Prime Video, for instance, allows the user to customise subtitles by choosing white, yellow or black on a black or clear background tag.

Subtitles must be syntactically and semantically self-contained, that is, they must not separate lines in the middle of a noun phrase for example. Segmentation or line break is the name given to the separation of lines in a two-line subtitle. Table 2.1 shows a correct and an incorrect segmentation or line break taken from the script of *Inglourious Basterds*

Table 2.1 Example of correct and incorrect segmentation

Segmentation/line break	
from the goddamn Smoky Mountains	goddamn Smoky Mountains
Example A: ✓	Example B: **X**

(Quentin Tarantino, 2007).

Example A in Table 2.1 presents a correct segmentation. As we can see, the line break appears after the verb phrase 'didn't come down', placing the prepositional phrase on the bottom line 'from the goddamn Smoky Mountains'. However, in Example B, we can see that the prepositional phrase is split up in 'from the' occupying the top line, separating the article 'the' from the phrase 'goddamn Smoky Mountains'.

Regarding the preferred layout of subtitles, Roales Ruiz (2017) supported the use of the pyramidal layout (the bottom wider and the top narrower) to alter the image as little as possible. Figure 2.2 shows a snapshot with this layout as borrowed from *Once Upon a Time in Hollywood* (Quentin Tarantino, 2019).

From the layout of the subtitle in Figure 2.2, we can see that it has the imaginary layout of a pyramid. This means that the top line will

Figure 2.2 Example of a pyramidal layout

alter the image less than if the pyramidal layout were inverted. This layout is not always possible, for which reason the priority is the semantic and syntactic balance of the linguistic and orthotypographic elements in the subtitle.

2.2.4 Text reduction

As we have seen with the technical constraints present in subtitling, text reduction is a must in this AVT mode. Díaz Cintas (2001a) distinguished two types of text reduction: partial, which refers to condensation because there are elements that cannot be included in the subtitle; and total, which entails deletion. Roales Ruiz (2017) reported that in subtitling, between 30% and 40% of the ST tends to be condensed in the TT, making essential the subtitler's ability to reduce the text.

Roales Ruiz's (2017: 62–73) stylistic strategies, which aim to condense the original or ST, are summarised as follows:

(1) Syntactic structures (Partial reduction):
- Aim at reduction when there is semantic, pragmatic and stylistic balance.
- Change complex structures to simple structures.
- Change passive voice to active voice.
- Use the active voice.
- Change negative verbs to affirmative verbs.
- Change temporal subordinate clauses to prepositional sentences with a temporal element.
- Avoid the use of two or more repeated or analogous verbs.
- Change courtesy questions to direct questions.
- Use the simple instead of the perfect tense, 'be going to' and its derivatives.
- Use short words for longer words.
- Use demonstrative, personal pronouns and possessives instead of longer phrases.

- Use simple tenses or nouns instead of nouns that refer to place.
- Combine two or more sentences.

(2) Syntactic structures (Total reduction):
- Linguistic elements that can be omitted in subtitling – the use of subject pronouns in Spanish, for instance.
- Pet words or phrases such as 'as well', 'actually' and 'eh'.
- Onomatopoeias, defined as 'the act of creating or using words that include sounds that are similar to the noises the words refer to'.[3]
- Emphatic affirmative or negative structures.
- Pleonasms, defined as 'the use of more words than are needed to express a meaning, done either unintentionally or for emphasis',[4] as in 'kick it with your feet'.
- Certain expressions that are used in short answers and are internationally well known such as 'yes', 'no', 'OK', 'please' and 'thank you!'.
- Expressions that are understood among pairs as they are used in both languages similarly.
- Words or phrases repeated in the ST with a similar intention.
- Recurrent repetitions of proper nouns or nicknames.
- Irrelevant repetitions.

To summarise, the subtitler needs to be able to transfer the gist in the subtitles, which often entails a reduction in the linguistic elements that are not needed to understand what the audio and visual channel are transmitting to the viewer. However, the reduction in certain elements can impact on the pragmatic meaning, for which reason the selection of what needs to be omitted is sometimes not an easy task.

2.3 Punctuation and Orthotypography

Other important features in subtitling are the punctuation rules for subtitles shown on screen, and orthotypography is of great importance here. As Díaz Cintas and Remael (2007) stated:

> [t]ypographical syntax, also known as ortho-typography, [is] the field that defines the meaning and correct usage of typographical signs, notably punctuation marks and various elements of layout that are used for separating, highlighting and clarifying written text. (Díaz Cintas & Remael, 2007: 102)

Following Talaván et al. (2016: 72–75), a summary of the conventions that subtitlers (who work from a ST into Spanish) need to consider to ensure that the viewer can read the subtitles easily and fluently is as follows:

- Triple dots (…) are used to indicate that a subtitle is not finished and announce the next one. Currently, these tend not to be used to mark

this continuation. However, when expressing doubt, a pause or suspense, they are usually used.
- Full stop (.) is used to mark the end of an utterance.
- Comma (,) is used carefully to indicate some pause, but tends to be omitted at the end of the subtitle, as this is an indication to the viewer that more information is coming in the next subtitle.
- Semi-colon (;) is not usually used as it indicates a longer pause.
- Brackets ()/[] are usually avoided.
- Hyphens (-) are used when there are two exchanges uttered by two speakers. Depending on the client, some leave a space between the hyphen and the first letter of the next word, but other times the hyphen is followed by the first letter of the next word. Also, some companies prefer the use of two hyphens, while others recommend the use of the hyphen only in the bottom line as it is understood that there are two exchanges in the subtitle.
- Capital letters are used at the beginning of an utterance, with proper nouns, titles of a film/programme, banners, graffiti, inserts, etc.
- Italics are used to indicate the speaker's voice is in off, that is, the character is not seen on the screen, and also with songs and terms in an L2, which are not recognisable in the target culture.
- Question (¿...?) and exclamation (¡...!) marks in Spanish should be opened and closed in accordance with the rules for punctuation marks, and there should be no space between the opening mark and the next letter or the closing mark and the previous letter. Also, there should be no additional full stop after a closing question/exclamation mark, as this would be a punctuation mistake.
- Abbreviations and acronyms can be used to reduce the number of characters, but their use needs to be exceptional.
- Symbols such as $, % and & should only be used when strictly necessary.
- Numbers from zero to ten are usually spelt out, that is, in words. While from 11 onwards, they are written in numerals.
- Time, measurements and weight are written with numerals followed by the unit abbreviation.

These conventions are not strictly used in all products, as some clients may have other preferences. However, they aim to provide the reader with general punctuation and orthotypography standards.

2.4 The Semiotic Dimension of Subtitling

AVT not only deals with interlingual – from a SL into a TL – and intralingual – from a ST into a TT – texts, but also resorts to two codified channels: the audio and the visual channel. Simply put, we are dealing with the transfer from a ST into a TT and a target culture.

Zabalbeascoa (1997) referred to two channels in AVT and then four different signs: audio-verbal (words uttered), audio-non-verbal (other types of sounds), visual-verbal (writing) and visual-non-verbal (other types of visual signs). These concepts, with slight modifications, were also supported by other scholars such as Chaume (2000) and Sokoli (2000). Thus, a combination of all the aforementioned elements, i.e. verbal, non-verbal, audio and visual, carry the same degree of importance in understanding the audiovisual text and its interaction. This entails a type of communication in which text users have to use their eyes and ears in order to assimilate all the pieces of information encoded in such elements. Following Zabalbeascoa (2008), both channels and signs interact with each other defining the essence of the audiovisual text.

Audiovisual texts are multimodal since both their production and interpretation depend on a combination of semiotic resources or modes (Baldry & Thibault, 2006). Such semiotic resources combine verbal information (written and oral) with non-verbal information, making the text a framework full of codes. Pérez-González (2009) highlighted that semiotics plays an important role in audiovisual texts if we take into account that language, image, music, colour and perspective are included in major audiovisual text modes. In addition, Pérez-González (2014) applied social semiotic theory in TS and established that multimodal theory identifies visual and auditory modes. Among them are three core modes: image, language and music, considering each has its medial variants. This system is organised hierarchically in such a way that every core triggers the activation of a number of related sub-modes. Thus, the multimodal distribution of meaning present in audiovisual texts can help when making translation decisions.

Another difficulty for the subtitler is to create harmony in terms of intersemiotic coherence and cohesion. Cohesion must be present between the information the viewer hears through the audio channel and sees through the visual channel (Chaume, 2004b). Díaz Cintas and Remael (2021) pinpointed the existing coherence between the audio-verbal information transmitted by the two channels and the information that the subtitle provides to the spectator. Contrary to what occurs in literary translation, for example, the audiovisual translator needs to create a meaningful message that accounts for what is taking place on the screen on the basis of the different types of signs (Zabalbeascoa, 2008) that make the audiovisual text.

2.5 Subtitled Products

A large number of products on the market – DVD and Blu-ray for instance – allow viewers to activate different languages when listening and reading in either the SL or the TL. For example, Spanish viewers can listen to the English SL of the programme and read the subtitles in the same language to learn or boost their foreign language, or they can watch a film in English with subtitles in Spanish in order to better understand the dialogue. In addition, there are other possible combinations, examples of which include listening to dubbed versions in languages other than the original, listening to a dubbed version in a given language with subtitles in another language or displaying primary and secondary subtitles in third languages.

In the case of current VOD platforms, the viewer can also choose from several possible audio combinations depending on the programme or film, and the choice is much more varied than in the case of DVDs or Blu-rays, which often offer fewer languages than digital platforms. In addition, the language combinations provided by current VOD platforms are extensive. For example, the TV series *See* (Steven Knight, 2019– 2022) on Apple TV, allows users to count on many linguistic combinations to suit all tastes – for dubbing, AD, subtitles and SDH – as Table 2.2 illustrates.

Table 2.2 Example of language combinations in *See* by Apple TV

Audio/audio description	Subtitles/SDH
Spanish (Spain) + AD; Spanish (Latin America) + AD; German + AD; French (Canada) + AD; French (France) + AD; English + AD; Italian + AD; Japanese + AD; Portuguese (Brazil) + AD; Russian + AD	Spanish (Spain) + SDH; Spanish (Latin America) + SDH; German + SDH; Bulgarian + SDH; Traditional Cantonese + SDH; Czech + SDH; Simplified Chinese + SDH; Traditional Chinese + SDH; Korean + SDH; Danish + SDH; Slovak + SDH; Slovenian + SDH; Estonian + SDH; Finnish + SDH; French (Canada) + SDH; French (France) + SDH; Greek + SDH; Hebrew + SDH; Hindi + SDH; Hungarian + SDH; Indonesian + SDH; English + SDH; Italian + SDH; Japanese + SDH; Latvian + SDH; Lithuanian + SDH; Malayan + SDH; Dutch + SDH; Norwegian + SDH; Polish + SDH; Portuguese + SDH; Portuguese (Brazil) + SDH; Russian + SDH; Swedish + SDH; Thai + SDH; Tamil + SDH; Turkish + SDH; Telugu + SDH; Ukrainian + SDH; Vietnamese + SDH; Arabic + SDH

From Table 2.2, which shows the order of languages in accordance with Apple TV in Spain, we can infer that dubbing is a more expensive process than subtitling (Díaz Cintas, 2001a). In line with this, AD is also an accessibility mode that entails more costs than SDH, given the number of professionals involved when adding voices to the audiovisual product. Moreover, we can see the large number of AVT modes and language combinations provided by VOD broadcasters if we compare them with the origins of video home system (VHS) and DVD products for instance.

Sánchez-Mompeán (2021) reported on data related to Netflix and Spanish TV series *La casa de papel* [The house of paper], titled *Money Heist* (Álex Pina, 2017–2021) dubbed into English. According to Parrot Analytics (Clark, online),[5] in September 2021, this series was said to be 'the most in-demand series globally across all platforms'. Sánchez-Mompeán (2021) highlights that Netflix has redubbed new versions to avoid the 'dubby effect', understood as a type of dialogue that is not convincing or natural for viewers. According to Netflix's own figures, for the first time, dubbing might be surpassing subtitling in terms of the AVT mode offered by the platform. Thus, we are witnessing important tendencies in the audiovisual market as subtitled language combinations in films and TV series have been more varied than those dubbed in the last few decades.

Returning to subtitling, as the AVT mode of study here, it could be asked if the work done by audiovisual translators is at stake because of automatic translation and post-editing practices as reported. On 13 October 2021, ATRAE (*Asociación de Traducción y Adaptación Audiovisual de España*) [Association of Audiovisual Translation and Adaptation of Spain] communicated on its website that the South Korean TV series, internationally known as *Squid Game* (Hwang Dong-hyuk, 2021), was broadcast by Netflix in Spain with Spanish subtitles, which had been created on the basis of automatic translation, being at a later stage post-edited. ATRAE complained about how precarious this sector could become and how bad the quality of audiovisual translations would be if this practice were allowed in the future. The association encourages digital platforms to communicate with their providers in an attempt to stop carrying out automatic translation to be post-edited, trusting audiovisual translators' skills and quality. It also suggests that viewers complain to the digital platform by using the tag 'inform about a problem', expressing their unhappiness about the product subtitled. We still do not know if this will be common practice in the next few years, but it can be argued that, to date, it is very difficult for machine-generated translations to compete with human translation in terms of subtlety and nuance.

2.6 Manipulation

As claimed by Lefevere (1992: xi), translation is a rewriting of a ST and 'all rewritings, whatever their intention, reflect a certain ideology and a poetics and as such manipulate literature to function in a given society in a given way'. Accordingly, manipulation can be carried out in the service of power. Rewritings can generate new ideas, genres and tools, and the history of translation is the history of literary innovation. However, rewritings can also restrain innovation, depending on the writer's ideology.

Manipulation can occur in the form of patronage (see Section 2.6.1) and censorship (see Section 2.6.3). Lefevere's (1992) view on patronage allows us to understand the elements that control the literary system in which translation functions.

As far as audiovisual texts are concerned, they can also be the object of manipulation, which Díaz Cintas (2012: 285) defined as 'the incorporation in the TT of any change (including deletions and additions) that deliberately departs from what is said (or shown) in the original'. Díaz Cintas (2012: 284) also supported the idea that manipulation does not always entail a negative connotation since, for instance, subtitling is determined by spatiotemporal constraints (see Section 2.2.1) and it is very common that dialogue exchanges have to be condensed to respect the technical restrictions, what the author understands as 'technical manipulation'. As already discussed, text reduction is a standard convention in subtitling. These technical constraints should not be seen as an opportunity to tone down or delete offensive and/or taboo elements in the subtitles, although this has been the case, especially in past regimes in which censorship was the norm. However, as will be seen through the proposed exercises, offensive and taboo language is usually subtitled faithfully into Spanish in the case of Spain.

2.6.1 Patronage

Two factors control the literary system in which translation operates, that is, professional and patronage, as Lefevere (1992) pointed out. The former is positioned within the literary system and, partly, assumes the dominant poetics. Among these professionals are reviewers and critics (who affect the reception of a work through their comments), teachers and academics (who make decisions regarding the books to be studied) and translators (who make decisions on the poetics and sometimes influence the ideology of the translated text). Patronage refers to 'any kind of force that can be influential in encouraging and propagating, but also in discouraging, censoring and destroying works of literature' (Lefevere, 1992, in Gentzler, 2004: 137). This second postulate then concerns the powers (both people and institutions) that can hinder or promote disciplines in literature such as reading, writing and rewriting. Lefevere (1992) provided a list of patrons as follows:

- Powerful and influential individuals in a specific moment in history.
- Groups such as publishers, the media, religious bodies and political parties.
- Institutions with authority to control the distribution of literature and literary ideas, e.g. educational establishments (national academies, academic journals, etc.).

The following taxonomy regarding patronage (Lefevere, 1992: 16) refers to the ensuing concepts below:

- The ideological component: The selection of the subject matter and the form in which it is presented are influenced by this particular form of constraint. To quote Lefevere (1992), ideology seems to be 'that grillwork of form, convention, and belief which orders our actions'. Patronage can therefore be said to be ideology related, considering that it is not limited to the political sphere. Ideology is the key

concept of Lefevere's theory of manipulation and considers whether or not ideology has been willingly assumed by translators or imposed upon them by patronage.
- The economic component is connected with payment to writers and rewriters. In the past, remuneration was carried out through regular payments or pensions from a benefactor. Translator's fees and royalty payments are currently the usual ways of remuneration. Patrons such as newspaper publishers, universities and the state can also pay or fund other professionals such as critics and teachers.
- The status component takes a number of different forms. The beneficiary of economic payment is usually expected to conform to the patron's expectations. In a similar way, membership of a specific group entails behaving in a very particular way that is supportive as far as the group is concerned.

On occasions, the three components explained above may be dependent on the same patron (whether person or group) – this is known as undifferentiated patronage – for example, in the case of a totalitarian ruler with the aim of maintaining the stability of the system. Conversely, the three elements may not be dependent on one patron, known as differentiated patronage. Audiovisual translators can share the economic component as they receive a sum of money for their work, but their social status is curtailed. In fact, in past decades, subtitlers remained invisible because many subtitled films did not even credit them (Díaz Cintas, 2001a). However, it seems that more and more current VOD platforms are showing the subtitlers' names once the film or TV series ends.

2.6.2 Ideological manipulation

In Lefevere's (1992) vision of ideology, translators can willingly adopt a certain ideological stance or another is imposed on them by patronage. Translators are more likely to have their work published or accepted if they are not in conflict with the ideology made by a particular culture. Unsurprisingly, ideology may impinge upon the choice and reception of the subjects of original texts in translation. When dealing with audiovisual texts, ideology can be equated with the norms imposed by the client upon the translator. With regard to subtitling and censorship today, we can no longer talk about censorial forces exerted by regimes in Spain. However, it seems pertinent to discuss the level of ideological manipulation that can take place in subtitling as follows.

Díaz Cintas (2012) referred to ideological manipulation as that which takes place when it is the subtitler who softens the load of some phrases or expressions in the ST. As written language can have a bigger impact on an audience than oral language (Díaz Cintas, 2001b), it is therefore common that in the case of religious referents that are vilified, the subtitle can show a milder or different version to avoid offending the target audience. This is very common with professional subtitling in Spain; the subtitler may 'avoid a faithful rendering of the blasphemy Jesus fucking Christ' by including 'some offensive terms to balance the load of this phrase, therefore avoiding a more abusive direct allusion to Jesus Christ' (Ávila-Cabrera, 2020: 128). Another level is the restriction imposed by the client on professional translators (Talaván et al., 2016), when they are given a black list of terms that are to be avoided in the TT. This usually happens with Disney productions, films edited for flights, etc., considering that some potential viewers may be underage.

2.6.3 Censorship

Offensive and taboo language has been subject to censorship throughout the history of literature, cinema, theatre and television. Over time, both the reasons and the censors have been diverse. Díaz Cintas (2001b) stated that censorship is carried out by dictatorships, governments, cinematographic laws, clients, TV channels, technical constraints and translators themselves through self-censorship. Censorship has been defined as 'the suppression or prohibition of speech or writing that is condemned as subversive of the common good' (Allan & Burridge, 2006: 13). In the words of Hughes (2006: 62), '[c]ensorship basically takes two forms, namely preventive interference by the state prior to publication, or subsequent punitive prosecution, dealt with more fully under fines and penalties and lawsuits'. Other types of intervention are exerted by the Press Council, the Church and self-censorship caused by cultural standards within a society, namely political correctness.

Far from the censorship carried out by dictatorships such as Franco's in Spain (Merino Álvarez, 2007), current social media are not exempt from censoring users who cross the limit of what they consider taboo. Spanish director and actor Paco León enjoys showing his nude body on Instagram. He is not exempt from censorship on this social network, and on multiple occasions, Instagram has deleted his pictures or censored them so that his nude body is not visible to his followers. The actor has complained about this censoring practice multiple times. For the promotion of the TV series ARDE MADRID [BURN MADRID] (Paco León & Anna R. Costa, 2018), some of the main characters appeared naked in single advertisements, but covered their genitalia with a tag reading ARDE MADRID [BURN MADRID]. We can observe how actors and actresses aim to defy a type of censorship they do not support. Another example is that of visual artist and photographer Sandra Torralba, who is one of the most censored users on Instagram in Spain. She supports the fact that Instagram allows for pictures showing male nipples, but every single female nipple on this platform is censored. In her case, she advertises her own artistic pictures that include erotic male and female nudity and, among the multiple actions carried out by her, she launched the sale of a T-shirt which reads #WEARMYNIPPLES, on which she shows her breasts.

Many other celebrities are censored on Instagram and other social networks, and there is no doubt that nude bodies are still taboo today. Celebrities are trying to break the chains imposed by this censorship exercised by social media. However, we can find the opposite to be true in the case of streaming platforms. Many of these platforms unapologetically break taboos for the benefit of the promotion of a TV series. In Spain in December 2019, Netflix advertised the second season of *Sex Education* (Laurie Nunn, 2019–). It was on the wall of *Círculo de Bellas Artes* [Centre for the Protection of the Fine Arts and of Public Interest] where they placed a placard which read '*querrás tragártela enterita*' [you will want to swallow it up].⁶ There is sexual innuendo in this announcement as *tragar* [swallow], in colloquial Spanish, can be understood in two ways. First, when one watches a whole audiovisual programme (i.e. binge watching). Second, when one refers to giving someone oral sex. A few days later, Madrid City Council announced that they had informed Netflix that the placard occupied more than 35% of the space allotted for the advertisement. Some days later, Netflix removed the placard (Cadenas, 2020). On Twitter, they tweeted the message '*hemos durado poco*' [we have lasted little time], which also contains a sexual innuendo. Was this a case of self-censorship? This tweet has had more than 8000 retweets and over 35 million likes, so we could infer that promotional strategies go beyond the limits of what is politically correct for the benefit of gaining more subscribers.

2.6.3.1 Why does censorship take place?

Censorship takes place when erotic, vulgar or inappropriate expressions or references are deleted or rephrased. Following Scandura (2004: 126), the most common reasons why censorship takes place in all means of communication (cinema and TV programmes) are described below.

Regarding politics, censorship is exerted by some governments as a weapon to prevent their citizens from knowing about other cultures that could represent a threat to the policies of that particular government. As for dubbing, some dialogue exchanges are omitted with the aim of concealing messages unfavourable to certain governments (Danan, 1991). As far as subtitling is concerned, given the difficulty in manipulating the acoustic channel, changes can be implemented through the visual channel. A case of political censorship in the cinema took place in China on 11 April 2013, with the release of Quentin Tarantino's (2012) film *Django Unchained*. As reported by Kaiman (2013), the Chinese media authorities cancelled the screening of the film, stating that it had been postponed for technical reasons, but unofficial websites associated the cancelling to a scene which shows Django's 'full-frontal male nudity'.

Political correctness varies from one country to another. For example, the sitcom *Ellen* (Carol Black, Neal Marlens & David S. Rosenthal, 1994–1998), set in the US and about a lesbian, was censored after a 'coming out' episode.

Religion is another powerful institution to consider. Alcohol is banned for religious reasons in India; some scenes of a US film in which youngsters drank whisky were reshot, using milk instead of the alcoholic drink.

Self-censorship concerns cases when translators themselves censor certain words or expressions for the sake of the target audience, determining what can be considered right or wrong. To illustrate this, in an episode of *Friends* (David Crane & Marta Kauffman, 1994–2004), broadcast on Sony Entertainment Television for Latin America, Monica and Rachel kiss each other in an attempt to get their apartment back. As the scene was not shown on screen, the translator manipulated the subtitles into Spanish expressing that the two female flatmates had kissed their male friends instead. The translator might have been instructed to do so by the TV channel or client, which is also common in current practice.

Other scholars have expressed different opinions concerning the reasons for censorship. For example, in the words of Lung (1998: 97), on some occasions, it is the translator's ignorance of a foreign referent or idiom that leads to a mistranslation, 'defined broadly as referring to any distortion of meaning as a result of misunderstanding the text, or a conscious decision to skip translating at all'. There are two reasons for such mistranslations in accordance with Lung: (1) ignorance of the idiom, as is sometimes the case with sexual innuendos, implicit in the ST, but omitted in the subtitles; and (2) ignorance of the foreign culture, which can lead to the failure to transmit the cultural context of the source culture.

2.6.3.2 Types of censorship

Censors can manipulate the translated text in different ways. Scandura (2004: 129–130) described the following types of censorship that are imposed on subtitling to a greater or lesser extent:

- Changing the title of a programme. A large number of translations of film titles are not faithful to the originals. Some people may think that this is an error made by the translator, but it is often a decision made by the distribution company. On other occasions, some film titles may have been changed by censorial bodies. Gutiérrez Lanza (1999, 2011) discussed many of the foreign films that were subject to censorship in Spain during the Francoist regime. Among the titles changed, *The Lady Gambles* (Michael Gordon, 1949) is one that was translated as *Dirección prohibida* [Forbidden direction]. However, current practice is to adapt the title of the audiovisual programme to

the audience and target culture. More than the translation of a title, it is a distribution company's decision.
- Changing the plot. The sitcom *The Nanny* (Peter Marc Jacobson & Fran Drescher, 1993–1999) about a Jewish American shop assistant who became a nanny changed the female protagonist into an Italian national, with the aim of fitting in with an Italian audience. In addition, the Jewish wedding was turned into a Catholic one. This is the reason why 'the "adaptation" was simply a euphemism for "censorship"' (Scandura, 2004: 130), ensuring that every Jewish element disappeared in the Italian version. This is a case in which certain cultural elements are changed, jeopardising the viewer's credibility, given the cultural manipulation that may become obvious.
- Toning down strong language. In the case of Latin America, translators are usually required to tone down offensive language, substituting vulgar words for neutral ones (Fuentes-Luque, 2015); for instance, the use of 'penis' or 'make love' instead of other slang equivalents. In line with this issue, Gambier (1994: 280) stated that the 'translator must respect norms of good usage (avoiding elements considered extremely vulgar or offensive if they appear in written discourse)'. This statement was supported by Scandura (2004: 130), with certain specifications, when she pointed out that 'extremely rude language should be avoided, but that does not mean we should neutralize and sterilize every single vulgar word, since in doing so we would risk producing a laughable effect'. This type of censorship may be controversial because of the conflicting views regarding the load that strong language must have in the TT. This can be explained in terms of lack of faithfulness; some viewers notice the ST exchanges are very strong, but in their subtitled form, they become mild. By contrast, Revoir (2011) reported that in the Danish series *Forbrydelsen* [The Killing] (Søren Sveistrup, 2007–2012), subtitled in English for the BBC, in 75% of the first season episodes, instances of the f-word were not toned down and, in fact, 25% had been added to the TT. The BBC asked to keep an eye on the number of expletives added and a spokesperson for the broadcaster pointed out that:

> whilst translation is not an exact science the important thing is that the subtitles represent the tone and sentiment of the dialogue as accurately as possible. At no point did the BBC ask for any strong language to be removed or toned down in The Killing II. (Revoir, 2011)

Authors such as Ávila-Cabrera (2015a: 54) posited that offensive and taboo language should be visible in subtitling 'so that the target viewers [can be] exposed to the same or very similar emotions, feelings and linguistic features found in the original dialogues and representative of a vital part of the characters' personal and cultural idiosyncrasies'.

Another distinction in terms of censorship was established by Santaemilia (2008), who placed emphasis on the varieties of censorship and self-censorship. Firstly, the official censorship supported by political or religious ideas is the type that took place in Spain, Italy and Germany under their respective dictatorships. These governments imposed drastic measures on every medium of communication on topics related to sex, political doctrine, religion and race. Secondly, there are other types of censorship that do not depend on external institutions, but are ideologically, aesthetically or culturally related within the hermeneutics of translation. In this respect, 'translators tend to censor themselves – either voluntarily or involuntarily – in order to produce rewritings which are "acceptable" from both social and personal perspectives' (Santaemilia, 2008: 222). This type of censorship is known as self-censorship and gives rise to different forms of omission and misrepresentation. Here, we could establish a parallel postulate with Díaz Cintas' (2012) ideological manipulation.

2.6.3.3 Censorship in the US

English literature had a long history of censorship interference before it came to an end in 1968 with the abolition of the Office of Lord Chamberlain (Hughes, 2006). Although the situation in the US appears to be more complex because of the rights preserved in the First Amendment, debates on censorship have continued on either side of the Atlantic with some authorities calling for the protection of their society's moral standards over the primacy of individual rights. Production routines differ from one market to another, and although the British film industry can be distinguished from films made in Hollywood, the reality is that many productions are in effect hybrid as filmmakers and scriptwriters have crossed frontiers, particularly in the case of British directors who have moved to Hollywood. Whether the films are mainstream, produced by the big major film production companies (namely Universal Pictures, Warner Bros., Columbia Pictures and Walt Disney Picture) or aimed at a smaller audience, as in the case of independent filmmakers, are variables that also need to be taken into account.

As described by Hughes (2006), the Hollywood industry has been affected by religious and capitalist control. The National Board of Review was originally founded in 1908 and censorship operated fully between 1934 and 1968, but after this period there was a large degree of free enterprise. The history of the American film industry is indeed characterised by the struggle between freedom of expression and censorship with bans made on topics such as 'the Cold War, the Vietnam War, race relations, feminism, and other political issues' (Hughes, 2006: 228). The main parties involved in the early years of the film industry were Hollywood producers and their opponents, who were censors and critics. Between

1915 and 1922, producers began to launch films with explicit love scenes, for example *The Truant Husband* (Thomas N. Heffron, 1921), prompting censors, under the control of the National Board of Censorship, to exercise more control over the visual dimension of the productions. With the arrival of sound in the late 1920s, censorship started to be implemented on the use of bad language too, considering that at the time films transmitted information prone to censorship not only through the visual channel, but also through the audio channel. In 1930, the Motion Picture Production Code was passed, stressing 'the MORAL IMPORTANCE of entertainment' (Hughes, 2006: 229). Certain topics were considered prohibited, such as sex, miscegenation (sex between white and black people), sex diseases, childbirth scenes and profanity (particularly using the words God, Lord, Jesus, Christ, Hell and damn). Adultery, passion, murder, crime, dancing, etc., had a negative impact on the moral conventions of society, although the film industry seemed to ignore such restrictions and still produced films like *Blonde Venus* (Josef von Sternberg, 1932), whose content was against the principles of the production code. The classic era of gangster films, which were very successful, started in the 1930s, with productions like *Scarface* (Howard Hawks, 1932). However, changes were introduced to the code leading to a significant reduction in the number of these films being commercialised and, by contrast, an increase in the production of musicals, costume dramas and biographies.

From 1934 until the abolition of the code in 1968, censorship focused on the political, social, racial, sexual and linguistic content of any American film. A striking change in attitude can be seen in the 1960s, when controversial films such as *Bonnie and Clyde* (Arthur Penn, 1967) managed to deceive the censorial forces to a large extent given that even though the film was criticised for its explicit violence, its script was considered clean. With regard to violence and political alliances, at the start of World War II in 1939, many films resorted to negative stereotypes and xenophobia. The end of the Vietnam War in 1975, signalled the production of numerous anti-war films with coarse scripts, critical of America, such as *Apocalypse Now* (Francis Ford Coppola, 1979), *Platoon* (Oliver Stone, 1986) and *Full Metal Jacket* (Stanley Kubrick, 1987), as highlighted by Hughes (2006).

In 1968, the Motion Picture Association of America (MPAA) (https://www.motionpictures.org) started classifying films, providing parents with information – in the form of ratings – on how appropriate a film would be for people of various ages (Hughes, 2006). Today, it establishes the following rates: G (General Audiences. All ages admitted); PG (Parental Guidance Suggested. Some material may not be suitable for children); PG-13 (Parents Strongly Cautioned. Some material may be inappropriate for children under 13); R (Restricted. Under 17 requires accompanying parent or adult guardian); and NC-17 (No one 17 and under admitted).

Jay's (1992) study on films released from 1939 to 1989 registered a dramatic and gradual increase in the use of bad words, and in this sense, the films by Tarantino, although written and directed at a later period, can be said to contribute to that increase and to constitute an extreme example of this tendency. In his films, all the topics – taboo, violence, drugs, sex, murder, crime, gangsterism, etc. – that had been the object of censorship in the past are mixed and combined with touches of black humour. Although it could be said that Tarantino has toned down his level of graphic violence on screen, as seen in *Once Upon a Time in Hollywood* (2019), he still preserves his spirit as a taboo breaker through his characters' violence and the swearing which his films portray.

Legido's (2021) recent study on censorship in Hollywood analysed 21 films that depict how the figure of the lesbian was treated in Hollywood and European films in the second half of the 20th century. In the words of the author, sapphic women were invisible, but this does not mean they did not exist. During Hollywood's Golden Age (from the 1910s to the 1950s), lesbian and bisexual women formed a group called the sewing circle, and had their own secret codes and parties. Among these celebrities were actresses such as Alla Nazimova, Dolores del Río, Ava Gardner, Greta Garbo and Marlene Dietrich. Even though homosexuality was not permitted in film dialogues and was not outwardly accepted among cinema stars, it was present. The film industry dealt with this matter by writing specific clauses into contracts. An example of the various films analysed by Legido is *Calamity Jane* (David Butler, 1953). Doris Day plays the role of Calamity Jane, a North American explorer who becomes an orphan and has to assume the role of head of the family and take care of her younger brothers. Surrounded by men, Calamity Jane manages to get along well enough with the men, showing her ability to ride, drink and shoot with the best of them. The way this character behaves, tells stories of Native Americans and dances in a manly fashion make the rest of the men accept her as another male. The audience can see how Calamity Jane, in all her masculine glory, feels strongly attracted to Katie Brown with whom she finally lives in a house. These two women play the role of butch and femme. However, Calamity Jane is not allowed to be a lesbian in the film, and Wild Bill marries her in the end, thus transforming her into a woman in accordance with what the Hollywood industry deemed acceptable at the time.

As described above, censorial manoeuvres were able to subtly hide different identities that for some reason were not welcome or accepted by Hollywood's industry at the time. Thanks to the studies conducted by scholars and researchers, readers can gain some insight into the story of censorship throughout the years in America.

2.6.3.4 Censorship in the UK

Censorship in the UK is governed by the National British Board of Film Censors, which was created in 1912 (Hughes, 2006). In 1916, a list of 43 topics for exclusion was passed 'ranging from "scenes laid in disorderly houses", "cruelty to animals" and "First Night scenes" to "excessively passionate love scenes"' (Hughes, 2006: 77), although there was no prohibition on the use of language. In 1951, the X certificate was introduced and the use of language began to be restricted. Until the 1960s, language, sex, crime and violence were restrained topics and strong content and style were systematically toned down. Most crime films were dealt with in comic fashion as in *Kind Hearts and Coronets* (Robert Hamer, 1949); sexual passion was usually omitted or idealised as in *Brief Encounter* (David Lean, 1945); and offensive language was usually missing in war films. On occasions, language considered indecent was hidden under the use of Cockney slang codes or double entendres. A significant film that broke the production code rules was *Room at the Top* (Jack Clayton, 1959), where the characters were seen swearing, cursing, committing adultery, etc. *Ulysses* (Joseph Strick, 1967) was a heavily censored film as two scenes and 400 words of dialogue were omitted, it was X-rated and, at the Cannes Film Festival, the soundtrack was replaced by subtitles. By contrast, since the 1990s, British-based films have been characterised by their showcasing of profanity and obscenity as in *Four Weddings and a Funeral* (Mike Newell, 1994), *Trainspotting* (Danny Boyle, 1996), *Trance* (Danny Boyle, 2013), among many others. Currently, its classification is U (Suitable for all); PF (Parental guide); 12A (Cinema release suitable for 12 years and over); 12 (Video release suitable for 12 years and over); 15 (Suitable only for 15 years and over); 18 (Suitable only for adults); and R18 (Adults works for licensed premises only), the latter being for offensive and explicit titles showing content concerning 'sex or strong fetish material involving adults' (https://www.bbfc.co.uk/about-classification).

Nonetheless, if Hollywood films are compared to British or European films, '[t]he persistent avoidance of profanity in the American cinema is an enigma in a nation without an official religion' (Hughes, 2006: 232), a fact that does not occur in Europe, in spite of the prevalence of Christian communities. The intricacies of censorship in Hollywood and the UK are relevant insofar as many of these films have been exported to other European countries, as is the case with Spain.

2.6.3.5 Censorship in Spain

Dictators such as Franco in Spain, Mussolini in Italy and Hitler in Germany are examples of the censorship that affected Europe (Santaemilia, 2008). Topics prone to censorship were related to sexual morality, political orthodoxy, religion, as well as racist considerations (Rabadán, 2000). Under Franco's regime, Spain was affected by the censorship of books, cinema, theatre and public events, as discussed by Rioja (2008). With regard to films, Gutiérrez Lanza (1999, 2007) analysed the manner in which censorial forces acted on English language films translated into Spanish from 1951 to 1981. The study is included in Merino Álvarez (2007), a collective volume of the TRACE project, carried out to investigate the multiple ways in which translations were censored in the fields of cinema, literature and theatre in Spain (1939–1985). The data obtained thanks to this research project give an account of the censorship imposed on narrative, theatre, cinema and television. However, while some films were banned or censored, others with similar features were not. This brings to the fore the blatant contradictions that took place at the time.

Gutiérrez Lanza (2007: 201–204) presented the dates and events that took place and are paramount to understanding the different actions that were carried out by censorship:

From 1939 to 1950: The Spanish frontiers were closed and the most traditional values started emerging. Franco's regime took control of the mass media and the organisation of public events. Institutional censorship started, including the Church as another active agent of censorship.

From 1951 to 1961: The *Junta de Clasificación y Censura de Películas Cinematográficas* [Classification Board of Censorship of Cinematographic Films] was created in 1952. Their main target for censorship centred on the dubbing of foreign films. It was the most popular AVT mode of the time and was prone to being strictly censored.

From 1962 to 1969: After a change of direction in the *Dirección General de Cinematografía y Teatro* [General Direction of Cinematography and Theatre], the classification board was reorganised, and new norms were set out on censorship that saw the creation of *Salas de arte y ensayo* [Rooms of art and essay], that is, special cinemas, in 1967.

From 1970 to 1981: With Franco's death in 1975, the dictatorship came to an end, giving way to a transition period (1975–1982). This was immediately followed by Spanish democracy (1982). Such deep social and historical changes allowed for the passing of new rules and regulations related to the classification of films, with previous regulations replaced. With Spain's transition to democracy, censorship was finally abolished, as confirmed by the Constitution of 1978.

From 1982 to 1985: *Ley Miró* [Miró Law], a law protecting Spanish films, was passed and the structure of the *Instituto de Cinematografía y de las Artes Audiovisuales* [Institute of Cinematography and Audiovisual Arts] was established. In 1983, X-rated cinemas were allowed to open.

Two boards were in charge of controlling censorship: the moral classification of the Church and the state censorship classification. The films censored by both bodies were rated (1, 2, 3, 3R and 4). The actions carried out by the censors included the temporal reduction of films, postponing the celebration of premiers and imposing restrictions on cinemas to broadcast certain commercial films. The work carried out by the group TRALIMA-ITZULIK (*Traducción, Literatura y Medios Audiovisuales* [Translation, Literature and Audiovisual Media], https://addi.ehu.es/handle/10810/34436) allowed for many lines of research into the way Spanish censorship impinged upon films made in English and dubbed and/or subtitled into Spanish.

Other significant studies on the censorship exerted by the Franco dictatorship are worthy of mention. Gubern and Font (1975) investigated the history of censorship in Spain from 1937 to 1974 from a political, social and economic perspective. Gubern and Font explored the views of some professionals of the Spanish cinema industry (producers, actors, film critics, censors, etc.) regarding what they experienced with censorship. The information provided by Gubern and Font (1975) was reviewed and expanded by Gubern (1981) highlighting the sociopolitical context from 1936 to 1975, the political repression exerted on culture and a comparison with other countries' censorship such as those in France, Italy, the UK and the US.

Pérez L. de Heredia (2014) depicted how harsh censors were with plays for the theatre during Franco's regime and how (self-)censorship was managed by theatre translators. A very interesting remark is that 'the conscious (self)censorship of the texts shows how translators are able to hide between the lines the politically committed elements, evading censor's work' (Pérez L. de Heredia, 2014: 705). One of the main ideological concerns of the regime was sexual morality and particularly homosexuality, both of which were strong taboos in society at the time. Other publications, such as that of Zaragoza Ninet (2018), depicted how Franco's censorship made efforts to stop any female thought that was not in line with Franco's ideology which included draconian restrictions on women. Many female writers were partially or totally censored both in Spain and abroad. This monograph deals with the link between the woman, translation and censorship, and censors' actions. All in all, it revolves around the disciplines of feminism, sociology, sexology and socialism.

Godayol (2020) has carried out extensive research on translation and censorship. Among her works, she highlights the achievements of the first publishing house in Spain, *LaSal edicions de les dones* [TheSalt Women's Editions], created in 1977 by a group of Barcelona's female intellectuals. Their main goal was to bring back texts written by important female writers of the past who had been forgotten, and also publish other female writers' texts of that time. It was indeed a rising project in a social post-Franco era in which the feminine discourse was gaining importance and the publishing house aimed to give feminism visibility. The project closed in 1990 along with other similar movements in Europe and America. Another example of novels and censorship is discussed by Gómez Castro (2020). American bestseller *The Betsy*, published by Harold Robbins in 1971, was censored in Spain under Franco's regime the first time censors read it. Then, a translated version carried out in Argentina under the title of *Betsy* was taken to Spain and censored for publication again. It was through a different translation that *The Betsy* was finally published in Spain.

Other studies, however, show how censorship was more permissive with some text translations than with others such as those for theatre and poetry, especially with classic authors. Bandín Fuertes (2011) discussed how the translation of Shakespeare's *Othello* for two performances, during Franco's censorship, at the *Español* theatre in Madrid evolved from 1944 to 1971, respectively. While the former version was an orthodox production, the latter escaped the power of censorship. Lobejón Santos (2013) analysed how censorship affected poetry translated from English into Spanish in Spain during Franco's regime. In particular, Lobejón Santos highlighted that beat poetry, which was published in magazines such as *Claraboya*, was less affected than any other type of poetry, probably because of its different norms and reviewing bodies.

As discussed by Díaz Cintas (2001a) and centring our attention on AVT, censorship did not affect subtitling as much as dubbing, particularly because the former addressed a minority audience, who, in most cases, could understand French rather than English, as French was the foreign language taught in schools at that time. Ávila (1997) explored the censorship exerted on dubbed films in Spain from 1937 to 1977. Ávila not only delved into the foreign films dubbed into Spanish, but he also approached the political, cultural and social events that affected the degree of censorship in Spain. His work provides readers with a selection of 100 index cards of the films that were the object of censorship from 1965 to 1977. This study also examines the censorial bodies as well as the numerous cinematographic laws concerning films from different decades, i.e. from the 1930s to the 1990s. Another study, conducted by Díaz Cintas (2019), concerns how Spanish dubbing during Franco's regime (1939–1975) was submitted to his censorial forces. Díaz Cintas examined examples from the film *The Barefoot Contessa* (Joseph L. Mankiewicz, 1954), in which Ava Gardner plays the role of Maria Vargas, a flamenco dancer, who goes to Hollywood to become a popular star. The author describes how the dubbing into Spanish of this Italian film shot in American English was cut three minutes. Among the scenes cut, we find Ava Gardner in her swimsuit while on a yacht and also her cousin (a gypsy with whom she was having an affair) visiting her. Furthermore, Díaz Cintas (2019: 10) highlighted the manipulation carried out on this film 'to such a degree that the dubbed and the original versions can be said to be two completely different films'. As can be inferred here, Franco's censorship affected not only the cutting of scenes, but also the dialogue exchanges, transforming them to the point of changing factual elements of the plot.

Censorship or self-censorship is not a thing of the past and even today, some of the types of censorship, although different from those discussed above, may still be in operation. Sometimes because the client wants to tone down the effect of some words in accordance with the potential target audience, and other times because, as we have seen, subtitling is very much constrained by spatiotemporal restrictions that force subtitlers to condense or eliminate considerable parts present in the ST. Additionally, we cannot ignore the fact that in Western societies, individuals may be self-censored in exercising their opinions because of potential retaliation from the mass media and academia.

2.7 Exercises

Read the following STs included in each of the examples and then try to subtitle them on the basis of the formal appearance of subtitles (Section 2.2.3) and text reduction (Section 2.2.4; Roales Ruiz, 2017). Although you do not know the reading speed, the duration of every subtitle and the number of characters allowed, try to use a one-liner or two-liner in accordance with the length of the script. These exercises follow a linguistic approach because in order to be able to subtitle them properly, we would need a subtitling program to reduce the text on a technical basis. However, you can pay attention to segmentation and try to make the line break maintaining a semantic and syntactic balance.

Note: Readers are not yet expected to subtitle offensive and taboo words and phrases in accordance with the aims of the book – these are the focus of Chapter 3. However, it is important that you start familiarising yourself with some of the subtitling conventions and be provided with a ST which includes either offensive or taboo words or phrases.

Exercise 2.1

Reservoir Dogs – DVD version

Context: The film begins with eight men in black having breakfast at a café, Mr White, Mr Pink, Mr Blue, Mr Blonde, Mr Orange, Mr Brown, the big boss Joe Cabot and his son Nice Guy Eddie Cabot.

ST: Oh, yeah, man. It's fucking great... You know what I heard the other day?

TT:

Exercise 2.2

Reservoir Dogs – DVD version

Context: The film begins with eight men in black having breakfast at a café, Mr White, Mr Pink, Mr Blue, Mr Blonde, Mr Orange, Mr Brown, the big boss Joe Cabot and his son Nice Guy Eddie Cabot.

ST: I know, motherfucker. I just heard it.

TT:

Exercise 2.3

Reservoir Dogs – DVD version

Context: Mr White has taken Mr Orange to the warehouse. The latter believes that he is going to die.

ST: The situation is I'm shot in the belly. Without medical attention, I'm gonna die.

TT:

Exercise 2.4

Reservoir Dogs – DVD version

Context: Mr White and Mr Orange review the steps for the jewellery robbery.

ST: If you wanna know something and he won't tell you, cut off one of his fingers. The little one.

TT:

Exercise 2.5

Pulp Fiction – DVD version

Context: In a club, Butch Coolidge, a prizefighter, meets Marsellus Wallace as they are going to prepare a boxing fight where he must be beaten by a knockout.

ST: Motherfuckers who thought their ass would age like wine.

TT:

Exercise 2.6

Pulp Fiction – DVD version

Context: Vincent is in his dealer's house to buy some heroin.

ST: And some dickless piece of shit fucked with it.

TT:

Exercise 2.7

Pulp Fiction – DVD version

Context: Vincent is in his dealer's house to buy some heroin.

ST: What's more chicken-shit than fucking with a man's automobile? Don't fuck with another man's vehicle.

TT:

Exercise 2.8

Pulp Fiction – DVD version

Context: Vincent goes out with Marsellus' wife, Mia, for dinner.

ST: Another way would be he was thrown out by Marsellus.

TT:

Exercise 2.9

Pulp Fiction – DVD version

Context: Mia, thinking she is going to inhale cocaine, takes an overdose of Vince's heroin powder. Vince tries to save her life with Lance, his drug dealer's help.

ST: I thought you told those fucking assholes never to call here this late!

TT:

Exercise 2.10

Pulp Fiction – DVD version

Context: By chance, Butch comes across Marsellus in the street. After Butch runs him over, Marsellus goes after him and they enter a shop. Butch starts punching Marsellus, but then both of them are kidnapped in an attempt to be raped. In the end, Butch releases Marsellus from the rapists and the latter lets him go with the condition of leaving LA.

ST: Now you just wait a goddamn minute, now! What the fuck you up to?

TT:

Exercise 2.11

Pulp Fiction – DVD version

Context: After Jules and Vincent have killed most of the youngsters and retrieved Marsellus' suitcase, Vincent accidentally shoots one of the youngsters in the face while driving and their car remains full of blood and brains.

ST: It means that's it for me. From here on in, you can consider my ass retired.

TT:

Exercise 2.12

Pulp Fiction – DVD version

Context: Jules and Vincent are at Jimmie's house where they will have to clean the car and get rid of the dead body. Winston, the Wolf, will help them do so before Jimmie's wife gets back home from work.

ST: I don't give a damn if he does.

TT:

Exercise 2.13

Inglourious Basterds – DVD version

Context: American Lieutenant Aldo Raine (Lt Raine) addresses his newly formed eight-man Jewish-American commando unit, known by the Germans as the Basterds.

ST: That's why any and every son of a bitch we find wearing a Nazi uniform… they're gonna die.

TT:

Exercise 2.14

Inglourious Basterds – DVD version

Context: Via flashback, the narrator describes Sergeant Hugo Stiglitz, who killed 13 Gestapo officers when he was a German private. The way he joined the Basterds is then shown.

ST: We know there's another Kraut patrol fucking around here somewhere.

TT:

Exercise 2.15

Inglourious Basterds – DVD version

Context: Lt Raine attempts to intimidate Sergeant Rachtmann since he does not give the German patrol away. As the German sergeant refuses to inform the Basterds, he is finally killed by the Bear Jew.

ST: About now I'd be shitting my pants if I was you.

TT:

Exercise 2.16

Inglourious Basterds – DVD version

Context: In a French village called Nadine, Lt Raine, his Basterds and Lt Hicox are gathered waiting for action within Operation Kino.

ST: You didn't say the goddamn rendezvous was in a fucking basement.

TT:

Exercise 2.17

Velvet Buzzsaw – Netflix

Context: Morf Vandewalt and Josephina are having sex in bed. He opens his eyes and sees a painting that disturbs him, so he has to stop. Josephina then expresses her lack of satisfaction because of this.

ST: We have a fucking problem literally.

TT:

Exercise 2.18

Django Unchained – Netflix

Context: Stephen, a loyal house slave, asks his master and plantation owner Calvin Candie about Django. Stephen is in awe seeing that Django is black and not treated as a slave.

ST: Just who the hell is this "n****r" you feel the need to entertain?

TT:

Exercise 2.19

Sweet Girl – Netflix

Context: Ray Cooper, Rachel's father, is seeking revenge against the pharmaceutical firm which pulled a drug from the market which could have saved his wife from cancer. Ray is threatening Vinod Shah with a gun pointed at his head.

ST: -I know there's others. -You don't have what it takes.

TT:

Exercise 2.20

Knives Out – Netflix

Context: Harlan Thrombey, renowned crime novelist, is found dead. Ransom Drysdale, one of the Drysdale siblings, addresses his sister-in-law, Joni Thrombey, disrespectfully over a family argument.

ST: Up your ass, Joni, you've got your teeth bit into this family tit so hard.

TT:

Notes

(1) 'The word deaf is used to describe or identify anyone who has a severe hearing problem. Sometimes it is used to refer to people who are severely hard of hearing too. We use Deaf with a capital D to refer to people who have been deaf all their lives, or since before they started to learn to talk. They are pre-lingually deaf'. Retrieved from https://signhealth.org.uk/resources/learn-about-deafness/deaf-or-deaf/.
(2) Interview with Díaz Cintas. BBC World Business Report, 10 January 2019.
(3) Retrieved from https://dictionary.cambridge.org/dictionary/english/onomatopoeia.
(4) Retrieved from https://dictionary.cambridge.org/dictionary/english/pleonasm.
(5) Retrieved from https://www.businessinsider.com/netflixs-money-heist-is-top-tv-show-in-the-world-2021-9.
(6) Retrieved from *El País*, https://elpais.com/ccaa/2020/01/17/madrid/1579283472_706278.html.

3 Offensive and Taboo Language

One of the gifts that human beings possess is the ability to communicate through language. The fact that there are over 6000 distinct languages in the world enriches the manner in which people communicate, although this fact can also complicate the way humans communicate especially when individuals do not share the same language or social class. Depending on the speakers' context, we make use of different registers, which Hughes (2006: 386) defined as 'a particular choice of diction or vocabulary regarded as appropriate for a certain topic or social situation'. We could ask ourselves: 'Why should we abide by the context when communicating?' In order to answer this question, I would like to highlight that conduct and rules of behaviour make our lives easier, allowing us to socialise with other individuals.

When speakers adapt their speech or choice of words to the context, we can see that there are a variety of levels, each playing their own role, since the words chosen can vary in accordance with the context. Murray *et al.* (1884, in Hughes, 2006: 387) present a taxonomy with three registers that move from the formal context, as seen in 'literary' (which includes scientific and foreign), to an intermediate or 'common level' (which encompasses technical and dialectal), to the lowest level, which is 'colloquial' (where slang is placed as well as any other words that belong to a low register). For the purposes of this book, attention will be focused on colloquial language, which includes words and phrases which can be regarded as offensive and taboo, as discussed in the following sections.

3.1 Historical Approach

Taboo as a concept is as old as humanity, and in order to better understand it, we need to go back in time. Primitive peoples associated taboo terms with magical words and also superstition. The term 'taboo' was borrowed by Captain James Cook in 1777, and 'came to refer generally to human experiences, words, or deeds that are unmentionable because they are either ineffably sacred or unspeakably vile' (Hughes, 2006: 151).

In specific cultures, certain taboo words are considered to be 'off-limits'. Historically, taboos have moved from religious to secular topics such as sex and race, 'but they can manifest themselves in relation to a wide variety of things, creatures, human experiences, conditions, deeds, and words' (Hughes, 2006: 462). According to Jay (2009: 153–154), these words 'are sanctioned or restricted on both institutional and individual levels under the assumption that some harm will occur if a taboo word is spoken'. Allan and Burridge (2006: 40) maintained that 'the phrase taboo language commonly refers to language that is a breach of etiquette because it contains so-called "dirty words"'. However, depending on the context, they can be softened through the use of euphemistic formulas, which will be discussed later in more depth.

In order to have a more general idea of what taboo entails, it is important to mention that every culture has its own way of dealing with taboo words or concepts. For example, Native Americans, Japanese, Malayans and most Polynesians do not swear. According to Corral Esteban (2019), Native Americans do not swear or, at least, did not use any swear words in their ancestral languages. In this culture, language is a gift from their Creator and, therefore, something sacred. The fact that swearing does not occur in some cultures may be difficult for Western cultures to understand as slang and offensive language are used to express anger, surprise, shock, etc. Here, let us draw a distinction between taboo language and slang. While the former can refer to language that may not be welcome, the latter refers to very colloquial words or phrases, which may or may not include swear words. Therefore, some slang words can be labelled as taboo, but not all slang terms are necessarily unwelcome.

Other types of taboos, described by Allan and Burridge (2006), are related to food. For instance, vegetarianism in the case of Hindus; prohibition of eating pork in Islam; food that can and cannot be eaten and the way it has to be prepared in accordance with the body of Jewish law, *Kashrut*; fasting by Muslims during Ramadan; prohibition of eating meat on Fridays among Roman Catholics to revive a tradition from centuries ago. At a different level, the casual or disrespectful reference to God is taboo in religions such as Brahmanism, Judaism and Islam (Hughes, 2006: xxi), and Christianity is no exception. Today, the concept of taboo generally refers to terms that should not be used, although this all depends on the speakers and the context in which they find themselves. Nowadays, the use of taboo words is related more to expressing something grossly impolite or unwelcome rather than strictly forbidden.

3.2 Terminological Concepts

Spoken words have an effect on us, and here we can define words that have the purpose of insulting, vilifying, or offending or can simply be more or less welcome depending on the other speaker's culture, age, social class, context, etc. Following Hughes (2006: 182), '[t]he use of terms like foul, filth, dirt, and dirty to categorize offensive or abusive language is profound and ancient'. In the past, words around the concept of filth were related to 'morally or spiritually unclean' or 'lascivious'. Today, there is quite a terminological disparity in this sense and there are authors who refer to this type of language as dirty language (Jay, 1980), strong language (Lung, 1998; Scandura, 2004), bad language (Azzaro, 2005; McEnery, 2006), foul language (Azzaro, 2005; Wajnryb, 2005), taboo language (Allan & Burridge, 2006; Jay, 2009; Khoshsaligheh *et al.*, 2018), rude language (Hughes, 2006), emotionally charged language (Díaz Cintas & Remael, 2007), swear words and taboo words (Díaz Cintas & Remael, 2021), among others.

Wajnryb (2005: 19) discussed the phrase 'foul language' (including swear words) and stressed the fact that it embodies the topics or issues that are usually considered inappropriate in social language. 'Foul language used in social settings can be equated with abuse or aggression', although it can also be used without directly insulting anyone. According to Wajnryb, two issues can lead to confusion when foul language is under discussion: (1) one concerns the swear words themselves and (2) the other has to do with the way in which people refer to swearing. The first point of confusion is related to the form–function relationship of terms used to denote swearing terms, so that there are more swearing functions than available swear words. Accordingly, the same words, similar semantically, but different pragmatically, are often used repeatedly. The latter point of confusion deals with the metalanguage of swearing, that is, the language employed in discussions concerning swearing.

If we look up the word 'taboo' in the dictionary, it is defined as 'a social or religious custom prohibiting or restricting a particular practice or forbidding association with a particular person, place, or thing' (The New Oxford Dictionary of English, 2001: 1885). Moving on to 'taboo language', O'Driscoll (2020: 31) supported that its nature 'has the potential to cause offence by virtue of it being normatively unacceptable'. As can be derived by both definitions, taboo is associated with what is considered prohibited and not acceptable. On the other hand, for O'Driscoll, 'offensive language' is defined as:

> any word or string of words which has or can have a negative impact on the sense of self and/or wellbeing of those who encounter it – that is, it makes or can make them feel, mildly or extremely discomfited and/or insulted and/or hurt and/or frightened. (O'Driscoll, 2020: 16)

As inferred by this definition, O'Driscoll emphasises the fact that offensive language has a negative reception because the impact of the words can be either insulting or frightening.

Throughout the book, I deal with what can be considered offensive and taboo in the following terms:

> Offensive language refers to those linguistic terms or expressions made up of swearwords, expletives, etc., which are normally considered derogatory and/or insulting [and] taboo language is related to terms that are not considered appropriate or acceptable with regard to the context, culture, language and/or medium where they are uttered. (Ávila-Cabrera, 2016b: 28)

It is not my intention here to criticise other authors' conceptions that refer to language used to offend, insult, abuse or may simply be unwelcome; in fact, I do not support the concept of offensive and taboo language as the only terminology to use. However, I will resort to the concepts of offensive and taboo language (Ávila-Cabrera, 2014) for lexical consistency in order to shed some light on its treatment when subtitled into Spanish in Spain.

3.3 Taxonomy of Offensive and Taboo Terms

To support the use of the phrase 'offensive and taboo language' (Ávila-Cabrera, 2014), let us focus on the following example. The word 'motherfucker' is no doubt an insult, and as such it can be considered an offensive term. However, there are those who could argue that it is a term that could also be considered taboo given its sexual connotation for which reason some words or swear words can be categorised in different terms. In addition, if we used the term 'have sex', we would be dealing with an act that depending on the context could be considered taboo or not. We could not say that this is an offensive phrase, but taboo, since talking about sex among friends can be a normal and welcome topic. Indeed, in certain contexts it could make listeners uncomfortable, but it would be a personal choice rather than a generalised feeling contrary to what happens when we hear a term such as 'motherfucker'. On the other hand, as happens with the latter word, the categories of offensive and taboo can overlap. For example, this occurs with the combination of strong words as in 'Jesus fucking Christ!'. The religious reference can be considered taboo because Christians do not use the name of 'God' in vain and this phrase makes use of 'Jesus' and 'Christ'. Then the addition of the word 'fucking' turns this phrase into a very strong and offensive one indeed. Thus, we can find multiple cases which are difficult to fit into a single category.

Here, I make a distinction between the two main categories of offensive and taboo terms. The following subcategories are based on the taxonomies considered by Wajnryb (2005), Allan and Burridge (2006), Hughes (2006) and Jay (2009), as expanded and proposed by Ávila-Cabrera (2014: 83). The aim here is to employ terminology that is suited to the specific purposes of the present study as shown by Table 3.1, which is based on the latter author and with further modifications. All the examples have been borrowed from films and TV series present in the book exercises.[1]

Table 3.1 Taxonomy of offensive and taboo language

Category	Subcategory	Examples
Offensive	Curse/threat/violence	If my wife dies, it's your death sentence.
	Expletive	Fucking hell!
	Insult	Bunch of shitheads.
	Invective	I wasn't speaking to you, Lieutenant Munich.
	Swearing	I swear on my mother's grave.
	Swear words/phrases	What the fuck am I doing here, man?
Taboo	Drugs/excessive alcohol consumption	When I left home, my brother started doing bad shit, drugs and…
	Filth/urination/scatology	Dog eats its own feces.
	Profanity/blasphemy	Jesus (fucking) Christ!
	Sex	Do you wanna suck my dick?

The offensive language category deals with terms that can be used for insulting, threatening, releasing emotions or just uttering swear words/phrases, and the subcategories include:

- Curse or cursing invokes the help of a higher being so that some evil will befall someone/something as in the expression 'Goddamn you'. In the past, some supernatural power was invoked when placing a curse on someone. Nowadays, however, curses can be regarded as threatening language as in 'Eat shit and die' (Wajnryb, 2005: 17). In addition, threat and violence within the language to inflict fear and harm are offensive too, as in 'If my wife dies, it's your death sentence'.
- Expletives are exclamatory swear words or phrases uttered in emotional situations to express anger, frustration, joy and surprise (Díaz Cintas & Remael, 2021). Expletives are not usually addressed to anyone in particular and their function is primarily to release emotion as in 'shit!', 'fuck me!' and 'fucking hell!'.
- Insults are words whose function is to offend the addressee. An illustrative definition of an insult is 'a disrespectful or scornfully abusive remark or action' (The New Oxford Dictionary of English, 2001: 948). An example can be 'bunch of shitheads'. Insults can have multiple forms as they can refer to ethnic, origin and racial issues, as for example with the n-word (henceforth, 'n****r') as in 'A man walks into

prison a white man, walks out talking like a fucking "n****r"'. The phrase 'fucking "n****r"' is a very strong insult in American English if not the worst. Other insults can be addressed to people's psychological and physical conditions. According to Bulthuis (online), 'mentally ill person' or 'person who is mentally ill' should be avoided and 'person with a mental illness' or 'person living with a mental health issue' should be used instead, considering that a person with mental health issues can have more features other than the mental illness.

- Invectives are subtle insults used in a formal context whose aim is to hide the offensive load of the word or phrase. They constitute an insult rather than a swear word, inasmuch as they tend to avoid the use of standard swear words such as 'fucking asshole', for example. They allow the speaker to be disrespectful towards someone without having to resort to more direct words whose tone is derogatory. For example, 'I wasn't speaking to you, Lieutenant Munich'; in this scene among the military, the speaker is addressing a German lieutenant by substituting his surname for a German city to make his nationality explicit.
- Swearing, in this context, distinguishes between two forms: formal and informal. 'Formal swearing is a ritual of social compliance and obligation: in marriage, in court' (Hughes, 2006: xv); this case cannot be considered offensive. However, there are concepts that are considered sacred when swearing, as in 'I swear by my mother's grave', which to many people's ears could sound strong.
- Swear words and phrases are vulgar words that can be used sharing the same function as expletives or with the aim of just making use of rude language. An example could be 'What the fuck am I doing here, man?'.

The taboo language category, which describes topics that may not be welcome by speakers or are socially restricted, concerns the various subcategories described as follows:

- Drugs and excessive alcohol consumption can be taken as a taboo topic when it concerns the person involved or people close to the speaker. In 'my brother started doing bad shit, drugs and...', this example concerns talking about the speaker's relative's drug consumption, which is usually considered a taboo topic and not dealt with other speakers openly.
- Expressions related to filth, urination and scatology can be unwelcome, as a social barrier is established which makes speakers avoid a direct description of them. An example can be 'dog eats its own feces'. In addition, multiple euphemistic formulas are used when dealing with urination and scatology, as will be seen later (Section 3.4).

- Profanity can refer to mentioning religious figures in vain, while blasphemy can be considered an insult addressed to the aforementioned figures (Ávila-Cabrera, 2020). In the phrase 'Jesus (fucking) Christ!', we have a double effect because apart from referring to 'Jesus Christ' – which in English can offend a Christian as a profane phrase – the derogatory term 'fucking' makes it blasphemous. I should specify here that the terms 'profanity' and 'blasphemy' are also used mainly in American English to refer to the act of swearing or using rude language.
- Sex, in its broadest sense of the word, can refer to different areas such as sexuality, sexual organs and behaviour, 'functions and effluvia from the organs of sex' (Allan & Burridge, 2006: 144). It is a very recurrent taboo issue because we can talk about it with our closest ones, but we would not talk about sex with people with whom we are not very familiar. An example with a sexual reference could be 'Do you wanna suck my dick?'.

Compared with the taxonomy shown by Ávila-Cabrera (2014: 83), I have excluded the taboo category related to death. First, because it can be included in the offensive: threat/violence subcategory when it has a threatening connotation. Second, because, even though talking about death can lead to the use of euphemisms, strictly speaking, the faithful transfer of expressions dealing with death itself are currently used in normal terms, not being taken as a subject off-limits.

To conclude, it is worth mentioning that the same offensive and/or taboo term may be included in different categories owing to the fact that English and Spanish have different swearing systems (Fernández Dobao, 2006) and modes with regard to this type of language. This is one of the reasons why subtitlers need to look for a strategy or technique to transfer the offensive/taboo load in the TT in the best possible way.

3.4 Modulating the Language Style: Euphemism, Orthophemism and Dysphemism

Every day, we see speakers who can modulate their language style in accordance with their audience, the context in which they find themselves and the age of those involved in the conversation.

Allan and Burridge (2006: 1) gave an account of the language style speakers can resort to when referring to different taboo words in the following terms: 'orthophemism (straight talking), euphemism (sweet talking) and dysphemism (speaking offensively)'. Between these three terms, two of the concepts that contribute to intensifying or toning down the translation of offensive and taboo language are dysphemism and euphemism. Both concepts play an important role when dealing with these features of language. A brief discussion on the three terms according to Allan and Burridge is given below.

Dysphemism entails the substitution of an inoffensive term for an offensive one, for example, using the word 'ass', although it is slightly vulgar, instead of 'bottom'. 'Fanny', for example, is a euphemism in American English for 'bottom' (Spears, 2000: 134); however, in slang British English, 'fanny' has taboo implications since it means a female's sexual organs.[2] Needless to say, there are significant differences between American English and British English when it comes to dealing with language considered vulgar. According to Hughes (2006: 142–143), other examples of dysphemism can be seen in the alternatives for words denoting incompetence and stupidity such as 'blockhead', 'bonehead', 'dickhead', 'not know one's arse (ass)' and 'couldn't organize a booze-up in a brewery'. Thus, dysphemisms are used to intensify the load of the words or expressions that speakers use given that they are considered stronger than others.

Orthophemism entails the use of a more formal term whose content lacks offensive or vulgar connotations. In other words, orthophemisms are more formal than euphemisms.

Euphemism, by contrast, entails the exchange of a taboo-breaking term such as 'Oh my God!' for an inoffensive and acceptable term, like 'Oh my Gosh'. Euphemisms are used in an indirect, conventional or socially acceptable way to refer to embarrassing, taboo or unpleasant issues. Some of them are very famous such as 'go to the bathroom', or 'restroom' preferred by Americans, who avoid using the word 'toilet', while British use it; other expressions can be said to be collective or unconscious. The euphemistic phrase 'four-letter word' is defined as 'a short word that is considered to be extremely rude and offensive'.[3] It can refer to words such as 'fuck', 'cunt' and 'cock'. Another very popular example is the euphemistic phrase the 'f-word', to avoid using the term 'fuck'. Words connected with 'death' are prone to substitution by euphemisms such as 'to pass away', 'to depart this life', 'to snuff it' and 'to push up daisies' (Hughes, 2006: 142). In order to illustrate this, an example extracted from *Inglourious Basterds* (Quentin Tarantino, 2009) reads 'I may be rapping on the door momentarily' which was subtitled as *como parece que pronto pasaré a mejor vida* [as it seems that I soon will pass to better life]. The Spanish expression is a milder way of talking about his imminent death given that a face-to-face weapon confrontation is about to happen in the scene.

Allan and Burridge (2006: 34) distinguished the different features of preferred language expressions such as orthophemism ('faeces') and euphemism ('poo'), while dysphemism ('shit') is the dispreferred language expression. Thus, the union of these three concepts is referred to as X-phemism. While 'faeces' is a more direct term, a speaker who wants to soften the tone of the term would use 'poo'. However, if speakers want to opt for a dispreferred term, they would use 'shit'. As a colloquial term, we can claim it should not be used in a more formal context. In addition, it is true that speakers would select an orthophemism or even a euphemism with the aim of not sounding rude or overly casual.

In short, '[w]hereas euphemisms seek to soften the impact of some horrific event or taboo subject by indirect language and calming metaphors, dysphemisms are starkly direct, macabrely metaphorical, or gruesomely physical' (Hughes, 2006: 142). Table 3.2 provides further examples of these three concepts, including both English and Spanish in different contexts.

Table 3.2 Examples of dysphemism, orthophemism and euphemism

Dysphemism	Orthophemism	Euphemism
Fuck	Have sex	Do it
Follar	*Tener sexo*	*Hacerlo*
Piss, have (Br. Eng)/ Take (Am. Eng.) a piss	Urinate	Go to the bathroom
Mear	*Miccionar, orinar*	*Hacer pis, pipí*

Based on the examples provided in Table 3.2, dysphemisms indicate that the offensive/taboo word or expression has been intensified (fuck, piss/have or take a piss), then orthophemisms show more formal and direct terms (have sex, urinate), whereas euphemisms show the opposite, that is, that the expression has been toned down ('do it' meaning having sex, 'go to the bathroom' meaning urinating or defecating). Some euphemisms make use of formulas that can sound childish or funny to our ears. Some examples are those that refer to dying as is the case with 'pushing daisies' or 'kick the bucket'.

In regard to appropriateness or offensiveness, both factors depend on a number of variables such as the context and the swearers' social class, age and gender. The degree of acceptance will also vary from one culture to another, which means that the subtitler will have to measure the impact of offensive and/or taboo terms on the target culture before deciding on any given solution. Furthermore, English and Spanish do not share similar linguistic swearing systems (Fernández Dobao, 2006) to deal with offensive and taboo terms. For example, if we compare the expression of surprise 'Fuck a duck!' translated into Spanish, the result would be ¡Que te folle un pez! [Get fucked by a fish!], then we can see how both formulas differ considerably among each other. In American English, the two consecutive imperatives are commonly used as in 'Go fuck yourself', while in British English some other expressions are preferred such as 'Fuck off'! or 'Bugger off!'.

Thus, the subtitling of offensive and taboo language into Spanish may require different strategies and/or techniques depending on the conversational context, the function of these types of words and the degree of offensiveness to be transferred to the TT. The intensity of the scene can also influence the subtitler's decisions when making use of dysphemisms, orthophemisms or euphemisms, addressing both the linguistic competence of the ST and the information transmitted through the audio and visual channels. Many solutions will be far from literal, which means that the subtitler must pay special attention to remain faithful to the ST, but also make use of idiomatic words. The audience of the product is a really important variable to take into account regarding the degree of offensiveness or the level of appropriateness when considering a solution.

3.5 An Approach to (Im)Politeness

It is important to understand how the use of offensive and taboo language can influence the listener in accordance with the speaker's intention because we have seen that different cultures have uncommon ways of interpreting social acts. Thus, it can be stated that speakers utter words in accordance with the context and the function these words have in the conversation. Hence, the importance of decoding the speaker's intention when swearing is essential. This section aims to give the reader a general account of (im)politeness surrounding the concepts of offensive and taboo language.

When swearing, speakers express their emotional state making the listener aware of it (Jay, 2000). The act of swearing is common and usually takes place in public places. It is part of a conversational act, but not the act in itself. However, it could be said that a conflict between speakers can lead to further verbal and even physical aggression in accordance with the speakers' cultural background, social class and especially the context. An example of this could be an argument between two drivers for some dangerous driving manoeuvre in which both of them get out of their car. They then start arguing and verbal aggression could take place by threatening utterances addressed to each other, until finally the situation could end up with physical aggression.

The dimension of society in different scenarios is important to take into account, and this can include a variety of norms, expectations, contexts and the way language is used. This is the reason why it is crucial to understand the cultural behaviour involved in an act of swearing, for instance, given that '[a]ssessing whether swearing in discourse is rude involves the difficult task of determining participants' identity, relationship, social norms, intentions and motivations' (Jay & Janschewitz, 2008: 269). Research studies have shown that certain neurological conditions such as dementia, Alzheimer's disease and epilepsy (Jay, 2000) can cause patients to swear openly even though they may never have uttered swear words when they were younger. As discussed here, an array of circumstances can lead to the speaker's swearing under different circumstances.

Depending on the speaker's intention to insult someone directly or indirectly, it is then the listener who needs to decode the speaker's intention or hidden message to understand if an insult, for example, is being uttered against them. In fact, invectives (or subtle insults) are a common subcategory of offensive language, as discussed in Section 3.3. When speakers insult, intention needs to be decoded and the words uttered can be more direct or with a hidden load in an attempt to be more offensive or subtler instead.

In order to understand the concept of impoliteness, Culpeper (2005: 38) highlighted that '[i]mpoliteness comes about when: (1) the speaker communicates face-attack intentionally, or (2) the hearer perceives and/or constructs behaviour as intentionally face-attacking, or a combination of (1) and (2)'. Thus, following this conception, both politeness and impoliteness are involved in the interaction between the speaker and the listener. This idea brings to mind the camaraderie created when the word 'n****r' is intentionally used among black speakers, as there is no intention to offend the addressee. However, the term 'n****r' would be highly offensive if uttered by a white speaker to a black listener (Dalzell & Victor, 2008) and nowadays using this word entails crossing the line. It can therefore be argued that '[t]he phenomenon of impoliteness is to do with how offense is communicated' (Culpeper, 2005: 36). To conclude this point, it is crucial to understand the speaker's interaction to know whether or not impoliteness is occurring. To that end, there must be an intentional attack by the speaker, and the listener must perceive it as such.

Some everyday phrases are politically incorrect. For example, a few decades ago, one could hear the Spanish homophobic phrase *marica el ultimo* [faggot, the last one!] used by children when playing a game on the street. Ye (online)[4] illustrates that in Spain there are racist phrases such as *engañar como a un chino* [be deceived as a Chinese], to express that one is cheated easily and effectively; *no hay moros por la costa* [there are no moors on the coast], when one wants to say that the enemy is not close; *vas hecho un gitano* [you look like a gypsy], uttered when a person is not well dressed; and *es una merienda de negros* [it's a black dinner], used for moments of confusion and lack of order. Additionally, offensive phrases exist that refer to people with mental disabilities as in the case of *eres un retrasado mental* [you are mentally retarded]. Fortunately, more and more people are rejecting the use of these expressions which are offensive, racist, homophobic and politically incorrect, and thus belong to the umbrella of impoliteness.

Allan and Burridge (2006: 91) described the use of the term political correctness back in the early 1980s 'in the context of affirmative action hiring policies, curriculum revision, speech codes and general guidelines for non-discriminatory language'. Allan and Burridge support the fact that the current meaning of 'politically correct' language concerns the concept of euphemism considering that the use of inappropriate formulas for naming and addressing are dysphemistic. Following this argument, we can conclude that a politically incorrect phrase is that which uses inappropriate language either because it is offensive or because it does not abide by society's rules of behaviour.

3.6 The Impact and Treatment of Offensive and Taboo Language

In the previous sections, we have seen that the translation of offensive and taboo language is a challenging and controversial issue that subtitlers must deal with considering the impact that these words may have on the target audience. A word or expression that may sound moderate, mild or culturally acceptable within a source culture or language may, on the other hand, cause a strong reaction in the target audience. In addition, further considerations must be borne in mind when translating offensive and taboo language such as the medium, the addressee and the related cultures during the subtitling process, particularly the target culture.

As different cultures do not always coincide in terms of social acceptance and sensibility, the same occurs with the use of offensive and taboo language, which varies in accordance with the speakers' social status, gender, age, country and language, and tends to change and become more or less accepted over the course of time.

3.6.1 A cultural approach

The manner in which a type of register is used depends on the characteristics of each language. Wajnryb (2005: 210–212) discussed how different cultures make use of offensive language. For example, Bosnian curses are usually centred on the family, 'may your children play in an electrical circuit'; the Dutch opt for bad health, 'krijg de ziekte' [get a disease]; Norwegians insult by calling their peers 'fucking Norwegian whale-killers'. In Iraq, when people want to make a deal, they 'swear on one's own moustache', which for others is like 'swearing on one's mother's grave'.

According to Hughes (2006: xxii), the use of 'son of a bitch' was more in vogue in American English than in British English. 'Bloody', however, was recognised as 'the great Australian adjective' as far back as 1894; and the word 'whoreson' has always been more confined to the UK. The worst insult in British English is 'cunt', although in American English, 'n****r' when uttered by white to black speakers crosses all the limits of offensiveness by far. As put by Hughes (2006: 326), 'n****r' in American English varies 'from extreme offensiveness when used of blacks by whites, to affectionate expressions of solidarity when used in black English'. Sometimes, we can see the subtitling of 'n****r' into Spanish as *negro* [black] and the load of what this word entails is therefore lost. The audiovisual translator then needs to consider by whom and to whom this term is addressed. In Spain, a very strong insult is *me cago en tu puta madre* [I shit on your fucking mother] or *me cago en tus muertos* [I shit on your dead family members]. However, these and other insults in

Andalusia, southern Spain, are commonly used as camaraderie phrases and friendly banter, hence the importance of knowing the target culture well. Therefore, offensive and taboo language needs to be analysed bearing in mind geographical and cultural contexts.

As far as gender is concerned, Jay (1992) concluded his study on the usages of swear words in the US by noting that men swear more than women and resort to more offensive and different types of swear words. This imbalance between the sexes in language use is particularly striking and can lead to instances of linguistic sexism. As Wajnryb (2005: 133) pointed out, the semantic field of terms related to men is characterised by a substantial number of neutral terms such as 'guy, bloke, chap, fellow, dude', etc. By contrast, those words used for women are commonly negative or sexually infused, for example 'bird, broad, bitch, chick, whore, slut, cunt, cow, mistress, crumpet, hag, shrew [...] vamp', etc. When women swear at men, they usually prefer words such as 'arsehole', 'dickhead' and 'prick'; '[n]one of these, however, compares with the evil that emanates from an abusive CUNT, hurled male to female' (Wajnryb, 2005: 137).

Ivarsson and Carroll (1998) highlighted the fact that both swear words and obscenities in subtitling, which were prone to censorship in the past in many countries, cause problems for translators. In addition, Ivarsson and Carroll (1998: 126) also stated that 'such expressions seem to have a stronger effect in writing than in speech, especially if they are translated literally'. Determining the degree of rudeness or vulgarity of the word/expression in question is a difficult task, especially when looking for an equivalent idiomatic expression in the TL. Thus, subtitlers must handle offensive and taboo language with extreme care and discern between the impact and the value of the word or expression, so that an equivalent word or phrase can be used that is appropriate and balanced in the target culture. As stated by Hatim and Mason (1997: 146) 'the translator acts in a social context and is part of that context. It is in this sense that translating is, in itself, an ideological activity' that takes place between a source and a target culture.

3.6.2 An approach based on audiovisual translation

Some scholars agree that expletives have a greater impact when they are written than when they are spoken (Luyken *et al.*, 1991; Mayoral, 1993; Reid, 1978), but it is Díaz Cintas (2001b) who took a step forward when he asserted that:

> [r]eading a novel plagued with swear words or sexual terms does not seem to produce the same strong rejection from the audience or the same feeling of being offended. The context where reading takes place must also be taken into consideration then. Although reading is ultimately an

individual act, it is not the same to read a book on your own, in private, as to read (and watch) a film as part of a gregarious group. (Díaz Cintas, 2001b: 51)

Díaz Cintas and Remael (2021) stated that taboo words and swear words in subtitling are usually toned down or even omitted owing to space and/or time constraints. The exclamatory function of this type of language can also contribute to the audience's understanding of a speaker's personality and idiosyncrasies. This is the reason why the deletion of such elements may not, in some instances, be the best solution. Taboo words are linked to local traditions and communities and are used differently depending on the social and religious environment, which means that they require a different translation depending on the context and the way in which they are interpreted. Taking into consideration the fact that swear words provide information about the characters and settings and contribute to the audience's awareness of what is going on in a specific part of the discourse, the deletion of swear words entails a loss of the communicative function of the ST as well as the suppression of the 'other', i.e. the man/woman who does not adhere to standard speech (Díaz Cintas & Remael, 2021). In addition, Santaemilia (2008: 227) suggested that 'eliminating sexual terms [...] in translation does usually betray the translator's personal attitude towards human sexual behaviour(s) and their verbalization'.

Swear words and taboo words contribute to the characterisation of characters' personalities and the fulfilment of a thematic function in a film or TV programme (Díaz Cintas & Remael, 2021), but their translation tends to vary according to the medium. Díaz Cintas (2001b) highlighted that films released for cinema distribution tended to be more daring when rendering swear words or taboo language on screen than films broadcast on television, which were usually toned down. However, nowadays there is less tendency to tone down or eliminate the load of offensive and taboo words on television.

Díaz Cintas (2001b: 65) argued that 'there are certainly differences between the levels of acceptance of bad language and sexual references in audiences that belong to different countries and to different social and ethnic groups within the same country'. In short, in order to subtitle offensive/taboo language, it must firstly be analysed within a certain context, taking into account addressee, target culture and medium. The function that this type of language has in the ST should also be visible in the TT, thereby demonstrating fidelity both towards the screenwriter and the characters portrayed in the films themselves. In Chaume's (2004a: 1) words, 'the main function of audiovisual translation is to produce a similar effect on the target culture audience as the ST produced on the source culture audience', from which it could be stated that offensive and/or taboo language should be rendered into the TT in order to produce the same effect that the ST does in the source culture.

Ávila-Cabrera (2020) described the importance of dealing with religious referents as part of a culture with extreme care. In the case of Islam, it is forbidden to portray Allah in art or literature. Naming a religious figure in vain is a sin for Catholics and has always been the case in Spain. Also, there are significant differences when referring to God or Jesus Christ in English and Spanish. A religious person, who is an English native speaker, will avoid mentioning these figures in a situation of despair, making use of euphemistic formulas as 'Oh my Gosh!' or 'Oh my goodness!'. However, it is acceptable in Spain to refer to God in a moment of despair with formulas such as *¡Oh, Dios mío!* [Oh my God!], although saying just *¡Dios!* [God!] would not be acceptable to Catholics as God's name is mentioned in vain. Then, in subtitling, sometimes we find the rendering of 'Oh my God!' or 'Jesus Christ' literally translated as *¡Oh Dios mío!* or *¡Jesús!*, but these are not balanced renderings since making use of the word 'God' or 'Jesus Christ' in the SL as an expletive is strong, while this is not the case in the given translation. Then, some different phrase should be used instead such as *¡Joder!* [Fuck!] or *¡Coño!* [Cunt!]. Valdeón (2000) pinpoints that while English tends to use euphemisms to avoid religious references, Spanish has fewer euphemisms for blasphemous phrases. On the other hand, in professional Spanish subtitles when the religious reference in English appears in the form of blasphemy, some other non-religious offensive formulas tend to be used (Ávila-Cabrera, 2020), thus avoiding causing offence to a religious audience.

Contrary to other AVT modes, offensive and taboo language can have a lesser impact on an audience when in oral form (Díaz Cintas, 2001a), as in dubbing. In this case, we refer to subtitling where the linguistic and paralinguistic information appears in one- or two-liners. Then, audiovisual translators need to search for expressions that are idiomatic in the target culture and language and can also transmit the message of the original script. This becomes a more challenging task when adapting that translation to the number of characters allowed on the basis of the subtitle duration and reading speed, as we have seen in Chapter 2.

3.6.3 Proposals for subtitling offensive and taboo language

In 2021, ATRAE (Association of Audiovisual Translation and Adaptation of Spain) published a style guide for subtitling into Spanish in Spain and its spotting. With regard to swear words and censorship, ATRAE mentioned the following:

- The ST must not be censored.
- Swear words must be transferred as faithfully as possible, making use of equivalent utterances when possible, without using them to excess. In addition, it must be considered that swear words in their written form often appear more offensive than in their oral form.

With regard to the impact that language has in its written form, already discussed by other authors (Díaz Cintas, 2001b; Díaz Cintas & Remael, 2021), we could argue that seeing the written word cannot be 'unseen', but one can almost posthumously mentally edit out a heard utterance.

The following are a number of proposals for subtitlers who are challenged with dealing with offensive and taboo terms:

(1) The subtitler should abide by the spatiotemporal restrictions of subtitling. This means that it would be preferable to reduce or even eliminate the offensive or taboo utterance in favour of respecting the number of characters used in the space of time allotted.
(2) The subtitled word or phrase should be faithful to the ST. Even though this is not always possible, some effort to transfer the load of the ST should be made to give visibility to the speakers' offensive and/or taboo words/phrases.
(3) The subtitler should take into account the intensity of the scene so that the transfer of the offensive or taboo language is not only linguistically appropriate, but also addresses what the audience is listening to and seeing on the screen.
(4) The subtitled word or expression must be idiomatic in the TT. A comprehensible rendering of the ST should be carried out aiming at naturalness in the TL even though the transfer of the offensive or taboo word/phrase cannot be fully materialised.
(5) The subtitler should not carry out a transfer of isolated dialogue exchanges. Instead, the whole ST must be transferred to the TT considering both the plot, the characters' linguistic features as a whole and the information provided by the audio and visual channels.

All the above recommendations I have elaborated are intended to help the subtitler in general terms. However, there are numerous cases in which the dialogue provides the subtitling with a myriad of challenges. Thus, these will have to be addressed based on more or less complex translation operations.

3.7 Research on Offensive and Taboo Areas

As already explained, a variety of terminology is used to refer to swear words, vulgar, offensive and taboo language. The following section presents different terms for the description of topics that share commonalities. In the last decade, an increasing number of studies have shed light on this less explored linguistic area from a descriptive translation studies (DTS) perspective (Toury, 2012), although if we compare it with some other areas in AVT, much research still needs to be done.

Firstly, this section deals with studies that, although they are not primarily concerned with AVT, have provided relevant insight into this linguistic register. Secondly, research on offensive and taboo language in subtitling and some of the more seminal scholarly studies on the subject are discussed.

3.7.1 Research on offensive and taboo topics

The anatomy of swearing was examined by Montagu (1973 [1967]), who documented the history of taboo words and phrases, delving into the genre with respect to its origins, philosophy and psychology. Jay is a world-renowned expert on cursing in American English. He has taken a psychological approach to sex roles (Jay, 1980), dirty language in the courts, in the cinema, in the schoolyard and on the streets (Jay, 1992), among others. His research on cursing (Jay, 2000) and taboo words (Jay, 2009) is extensive.

The fact that the use of bad language and slang is possible in standard English was analysed by Andersson and Trudgill (1990). Allan and Burridge (1991, 2006) dealt with euphemisms, dysphemisms and forbidden words. Their valuable work depicts the concept of taboos and their origins, carrying out a taxonomy based on the language for taboo topics such as naming and addressing, sex and bodily effluvia, food and smell, disease, death and killing, and the censoring around taboo language. Valdeón (2000) conducted a study on taboo subjects, offensive language and euphemisms used in English and Spanish. The researcher administered a survey to Spanish university students of English as a foreign language on terms that could be considered taboo, one of the main goals was to make them aware of the words that could be considered inappropriate under certain circumstances in order to avoid having a negative impact on speakers.

Hughes (2006) is the author of *The Encyclopaedia of Swearing and the Social History of Oaths, Profanity, Foul Language and Ethnic Insults in the English-Speaking World*. This encyclopaedia is a must for any reader keen on understanding the broad sense of swearing and its evolution throughout the years. Indeed, it is a volume with which the reader can gain insight into the etymology of swear words, phrases and other words that are unwelcome to conservative people's ears.

The Lancaster Corpus of Abuse (LCA) is a research project based on the British National Corpus (BNC), a spoken corpus that contains bad language entries arranged according to the speakers' sex, age and social class (McEnery, 2006). This work deals with censoring measures on bad language and how this type of language is associated with age, gender, education and social class. McEnery maintains that current attitudes towards bad language in modern English are inherited from the late 17th and early 18th centuries, although this has changed even more in the present time given the use of bad language in different contexts.

O'Driscoll (2020) explored offensive language from a pragmatics and sociolinguistics approach. An array of examples which account for potential offence and actual offence are presented and function as case studies. In O'Driscoll's view, there is a thin line between free speech and criminal activity, and he looks into a new approach to offensive language in which it is important to understand how offensive utterances occur, the degree of offensiveness and the tolerance and empathy among the participants involved in the communicative interaction.

3.7.2 Offensive and taboo language in subtitling

The way offensive and taboo language is subtitled is a topic that has attracted considerable debate. On the one hand, some scholars in the past supported the idea that excessive offensive and taboo language had to be toned down in subtitling (Gambier, 1994; Ivarsson & Carrol, 1998), owing to the fact that written words have a greater impact on an audience than oral speech (Díaz Cintas, 2001b; Luyken et al., 1991; Reid, 1978). Others, such as Scandura (2004), maintain the idea that extremely offensive language should be avoided, but do not support the neutralisation of every instance of swearing. Díaz Cintas and Remael (2007, 2021) noted that the omission of emotionally charged language or swear words usually occurs in cases of spatial and temporal constraints although omission of this type of language also happens at other times, when it is not deemed to be the best solution. Chaume (2004b), for his part, discussed the fact that vulgar language should be translated for the target audience in such a way as to produce the same effect as these terms had on the source audience. More recent studies show that the load of offensive and taboo terms tends to be faithful to the ST 'so that the target viewers are exposed to the same or very similar emotions, feelings and linguistic features found in the original dialogues and representative of a vital part of the characters' personal and cultural idiosyncrasies' (Ávila-Cabrera, 2015a: 54).

It is not the purpose of this section to include every single study on offensive, taboo, vulgar language, swear words, etc. However, some relevant research studies that have similar features to the areas explored throughout the book are referenced here.

As an introduction to distinguish between different varieties of Spanish, let us focus on Fuentes-Luque (2015), who analysed the differences when subtitling and dubbing taboo language from English into Spanish in the case of Spain and Latin America. This author highlighted that in Latin America euphemistic formulas are the norm in AVT. This is a significant feature considering that the load of offensive and taboo language tends to be transferred more faithfully in the case of Spain, with some exceptions such as direct insults on religious figures (Ávila-Cabrera, 2020), which tend to be substituted for other offensive terms in the case of subtitling, avoiding a stronger impact on the audience.

As far as sex as a taboo topic is concerned, Lung (1998) reported that before the 21st century, English films and TV series started to include sexual content and tended to be under-translated in English-Chinese subtitles for videotapes. In some cases, this was because the translator was not aware of the English idiomatic usage, and other times because the translator toned down the sexual connotation for sociopsychological, cultural and euphemistic reasons. By contrast, Díaz Cintas (2001b) explored sexual language in the English subtitles of the film *La flor de mi secreto* [The Flower of My Secret] (Pedro Almodóvar, 1995) in the VHS version and the British version for Channel 4. The author called attention to the fact that the subtitles in the television version were more daring than those of the VHS version, probably because the latter was intended for the American market. Zabalbeascoa (2016) analysed Vladimir Nabokov's (1955) and Stanley Kubrick's (1962) *Lolita*, and the subsequent version by Adrian Lyne (1997), that is, the book and the two film adaptations, respectively, in terms of their humorous nature, sex and taboo. The author stated that Lyne's was a more faithful version of the book, while Kubrick's was categorised as comedy. In addition, Kubrick depicted sex and taboo in the form of words and images, but Lyne was more explicit in visual terms. Zabalbeascoa analysed a number of subtitled versions in Spanish and German. Among the conclusions drawn was that some possible errors may represent a type of censorship, different from those imposed by other authoritative forces. Finally, Bucaria (2017) analysed a number of US series subtitled, fansubbed and dubbed into Italian. Her focus was on taboo topics such as sex, drugs, disability and death. Among her findings, Bucaria stated that dubbed Italian versions tended to be toned down as opposed to fansubbed or professionally subtitled versions.

Regarding racist insults, Filmer (2012) compared the different cultures of the US and Italy to look into derogatory racial examples taken from *Gran Torino* (Clint Eastwood, 2008). In her study of the subtitling and dubbing of this film into Italian, Filmer concluded that racist insults seemed to be handled with a lack of alternatives in the TT, making use of more neutral options. In addition, the author stated that in domesticated programmes, racial slurs are not enough when it comes to depicting offence in the Italian TT, and to compensate for this, the translators resort to the foregrounding of homophobic insults. Martínez Sierra (2017) looked into the translation of the racist term 'n****r' in *Django Unchained* (Quentin Tarantino, 2012) for the dubbed and subtitled versions into European Spanish. Martínez Sierra conducted a descriptive analysis of the number of instances this term appeared in both versions and also triangulated data with an interview with the audiovisual translator, Quico Rovira-Beleta. In a large percentage of cases, the word 'n****r' was translated as *negro* [black], for which reason the author highlighted a case study in which ideological manipulation in the form of self-censorship took place.

The subtitling into European Spanish of some of the most popular films by Quentin Tarantino were analysed by Ávila-Cabrera (2014, 2015a, 2015b, 2015c, 2016a, 2016b, 2017, 2020). According to this research, as case studies, the first subtitles for the films directed by this cult director do not seem to be totally faithful to the original, although they exhibit high percentages of the load of offensive and taboo language. In the case of the film *Inglourious Basterds* (2007), the author interviewed its subtitler Arturo Enríquez García, who acknowledged his attempt to be as faithful as possible to the ST as far as the transfer of offensive and taboo terms was concerned. It is true, nonetheless, that with the passing of time, the subtitles are closer to the ST. This tendency preserves the presence of offensive and taboo utterances in the subtitles, allowing the audience to view a product with room for insults, swear words, taboo expressions, etc. In line with the study on Quentin Tarantino's films, Soler Pardo (2015) researched the swearing into Spanish of eight films. Her initial hypothesis was that insults from English into European Spanish in dubbing tended to vanish. After a rigorously detailed analysis of all the instances found, she shed light on the most recurrent categories and the omissions of insults carried out in the TT. By contrast, in a study conducted by Valdeón (2020), based on pragmatics and translation studies (TS), the author scrutinised four seasons of four different series, a grand total of 47 episodes, dubbed from English into European Spanish. The findings revealed that the presence of swear words in the TT increased (through the strategies of addition, the substitution of neutral words for swear words and intensification) in more than 50% of the cases, what the author calls the 'vulgarization hypothesis'. This leads us to observe significant differences between dubbing and subtitling, the two major AVT modes which are technically very different from one another.

Xavier (2021) has devoted her research to the subtitling of taboo words into Portuguese. She presented a model of analysis based on translation norms, analysing a corpus composed of Portuguese free-to-air, open signal films for television broadcast between 2001 and 2015, in English subtitled into Portuguese. The quantitative data were triangulated with qualitative data provided by audiovisual translators on the way they dealt with taboo words subtitled into Portuguese for television. Among the findings are the norm of euphemising operations and the norm of valuing omission.

Al-Adwan's (2015) study centred on the use of euphemisation – as a politeness strategy – in subtitling the tenth season of the series *Friends* (David Crane & Marta Kauffman, 1994–2004), that is, from American English into Arabic. Based on Levinson's (1983) theory of politeness, the author explored the way translators subtitle taboo topics such as sex and others related to death, disease and bodily functions by means of euphemistic formulas. Izwaini (2018) discussed the role of censorship in Arabic subtitles. The manipulation of subtitles is dependent on adapting to the norms of the target culture as well as cultural sensitiveness, which leads to the toning down and neutralising of vulgar language in favour of utilising non-offensive or sanitised formulas. The examples evaluated were on topics about religion (God), sexual references (body parts), alcohol and drugs, social designations and other offensive topics (Izwaini, 2017b). Khoshsaligheh et al. (2018) delved into the translation into Persian of films in English by fansubbers. The focus was on taboo language and the findings were quite revealing as the techniques used by the fansubbers, as found by the researchers, were those that preserve the transfer of the load of taboo language. Instead of resorting to norms present in Iranian society, whose ideology is conservative, they considered the source culture norms instead. Alsharhan (2020) conducted a study about the no-censorship policy established by Netflix to subtitle taboo language from English into Arabic. Alsharhan analysed five programmes broadcast by Netflix with ample taboo language instances along with a taxonomy of the strategies employed by the subtitlers. Among her findings, Alsharhan highlights the fact that a variety of strategies were used instead of just omission and other euphemistic formulas, common in these linguistic combinations. Another relevant result is that even though Netflix's policy was aimed at no censorship, half of the taboo language instances were euphemised.

Experimental studies of taboo topics and AVT on undergraduates have also been conducted. Valdeón (2015) analysed the outcome of two groups of advanced English students who had to translate two episodes of the series *The IT Crowd* (Graham Linehan, 2006–2013) into Spanish. Their translations were then compared with the dubbed versions. Among the results encountered, it was found that while the students toned down the swear words in the TT, the translators maintained the load of these words, even increasing it. Ávila-Cabrera and Rodríguez Arancón (2018) also conducted a study with undergraduates. Students from the National Distance Education University (UNED) had to subtitle several film clips from English into Spanish and vice versa. The focus was on the (un)faithfulness to the load of offensive and taboo terms; however, in an attempt to not influence the goal of the study, the students were unaware of this fact. The results proved that the English-Spanish subtitles were mostly faithful to the ST. However, in the case of the Spanish-English subtitles, the results were even more daring (or offensive). This result could suggest that when using a foreign language, speakers have fewer cultural constraints which can lead them to feel freer when swearing. Another significant datum was that when dealing with blasphemies, students tended to neutralise them or maintain an offensive load, but without using religious figures. This finding has commonalities with the results found by

Ávila-Cabrera (2020) on the subtitling into European Spanish of religious figures in Tarantino's films.

Parra López's (2019) thesis, which opens a new avenue of research into AVT, concerns what he refers to as disorderly speech. In this study, the author analysed a number of films in English dubbed and subtitled into Spanish in which the characters' linguistic features were influenced by the use of drugs and alcohol. The approach taken was based on language variation, fictional orality, style and multilingualism. This is a taboo topic that had not been previously researched, and which can provide fruitful insight into the literature of taboo topics and AVT.

The studies listed in this section come from a range of disciplines and have influenced, to some extent, the research I have conducted on offensive and/or taboo language within AVT.

3.8 Exercises

The following charts are intended to enable the reader to practice with words that can be considered offensive or taboo. To that aim, it is suggested that the reader fill in the missing cells in accordance with their label, that is, dysphemism, orthophemism and euphemism. One of the cells is given along with its translation into Spanish and the remaining ones must be written in English with their translation or equivalent in Spanish as well.

Part 1

Complete the following charts in English and Spanish by filling in the missing dysphemism, orthophemism and/or euphemism of the given words.

Exercise 3.1

Fill in the missing words/phrases related to offensive expletives.

Dysphemism	Orthophemism	Euphemism
Fuck!		
¡Joder!		
	Oops!	
	¡Oh!	
Fucking hell!		
¡Coño!		
		What the heck!
		¡Me cachis (en la mar)!

Exercise 3.2

Fill in the missing words/phrases related to physiological functions.

Dysphemism	Orthophemism	Euphemism
Crapper (Br. Eng.)/ Shitter (Am. Eng.)		
Cagadero		
	Urinate	
	Miccionar/Orinar	
		Go to the bathroom/ Have a bowel movement/ Drop the kids off the pool
		Ir al baño/ Hacer de vientre, cuerpo/ Plantar un pino
	Break wind/Pass gas	
	Ventosear	

Exercise 3.3

Fill in the missing words/phrases related to sex.

Dysphemism	Orthophemism	Euphemism
		Do it
		Hacerlo
	Fornicate	
	Fornicar	
Eat pussy		
Comer el coño		
	Fellatio	
	Felación/Sexo oral	

Exercise 3.4

Fill in the missing words/phrases related to death and mental illness.

Dysphemism	Orthophemism	Euphemism
Die		
Morir		
	Live with a mental illness	
	Padecer depresión	
		Challenged/Special
		Paticojo/a
	Vomit	
	Vomitar	

Exercise 3.5

Fill in the missing words/phrases related to religion.

Dysphemism	Orthophemism	Euphemism
		Oh my Gosh!/ Oh my goodness!
		¡Maldita sea!/ ¡Maldición!
Holy shit!		
¡Hostia puta!		
	Good Lord!	
	¡Por el amor de Dios!/ ¡Vaya por Dios!	

Exercise 3.6

Fill in the missing words/phrases related to race, sexual conditions and insults.

Dysphemism	Orthophemism	Euphemism
'N****r'/Negro/a		
Negrata/Negro/a de mierda		
	Lesbian	
	Lesbiana	
		Gay
		Mariquita/Mariflor
Whore/Hooker		
Puta		
		Gigolo
		Gigoló

Part 2

Subtitle the following dialogue exchanges into Spanish carrying out proper segmentation. Also, pay attention to the words in bold type from the ST and specify what category we are dealing with – offensive or taboo – and its subcategory.

Note: In real practice, the whole ST should be available to the subtitler because this professional practice entails taking into account both the complete ST and the information provided by the audio and visual channel. However, the exercises presented here are aimed at practising possible renderings of some challenging expressions which have offensive and/or taboo words.

Exercise 3.7

The Hateful Eight – DVD version

Context: Major Marquis tells General Sandy Smithers how he made his son suffer before killing him naked in the snow.

ST: and I stuck **my big, black Johnson** right down his goddamn throat.

TT:

Category/subcategory:

Exercise 3.8

Reservoir Dogs – DVD version

Context: Mr Blonde enters the warehouse and more arguments and quarrelling ensue.

ST: You're acting like **a bunch of fucking "n****rs"**, man!

TT:

Category/subcategory:

Exercise 3.9

Nine Perfect Strangers SE01 EP05 – Prime Video

Context: While having breakfast at the table, Lars Lee tells everyone about a strange dream he had. Lars says Tony Hogburn was in it and receives the following reply.

ST: -You're **a fucking lunatic**. You know that, Lars? -Yeah, I know.

TT:

Category/subcategory:

Exercise 3.10

Pulp Fiction – DVD version

Context: A young man with an English accent and his girlfriend are sitting in an LA coffee shop where they will try to rob all the customers and employees.

ST: Normally **both your asses** would be **dead as fucking fried chicken**.

TT:

Category/subcategory:

Exercise 3.11

Succession SE03 EP09 – HBO

Context: The Roy siblings are in Italy for their mother's wedding. Also present is their father and CEO of the firm, Logan Roy. Tom Wambsgans, Shiv's husband, is talking to Greg Hirsch disrespectfully.

ST: "Uh, but I don't recall, Your Honor, I don't recall…". **You're a fucking joke**, man.

TT:

Category/subcategory:

Exercise 3.12

Inglourious Basterds – DVD version

Context: In a French village called Nadine, Lt Raine, his Basterds and Lt Hicox are gathered waiting for action within Operation Kino.

ST: This **Jerry** of yours, Stiglitz, not exactly the **loquacious** type, is he?

TT:

Category/subcategory:

Exercise 3.13

Pulp Fiction – DVD version

Context: In a club, Butch Coolidge, a prizefighter, meets Marsellus Wallace as they are going to prepare a boxing fight where he must be beaten by a knockout.

ST: When you kicking it in the Caribbean,

TT:

Category/subcategory:

Exercise 3.14

Narcos: Mexico SE03 EP05 – Netflix

Context: DEA agent Walt Breslin is talking to other agents about the Mexican Cartels and then he reacts after some information is given to the group.

ST: Are you **fucking** kidding me?

TT:

Category/subcategory:

Exercise 3.15

Once Upon a Time in Hollywood – DVD version

Context: Rick Dalton and his stunt double Cliff Booth are driving. They stop at a traffic light and Rick insults a group of hippies he sees on the street.

ST: **Fucking** hippie **motherfuckers**.

TT:

Category/subcategory:

Exercise 3.16

Once Upon a Time in Hollywood – DVD version

Context: Rick Dalton has a conversation with filmmaker Sam Wanamaker.

ST: -**Goddamn it. I fucked this whole thing up**, Sam. -Keep going.

TT:

Category/subcategory:

Exercise 3.17

The White Lotus SE01 EP01 – HBO

Context: On a boat trip in Hawaii, Olivia Mossbacher and her friend Paula fantasise about the lives of the recently married couple Shane and Rachel Patton.

ST: -She loves him, but... -He's got a **small dick**.

TT:

Category/subcategory:

Exercise 3.18

Succession SE03 EP09 – HBO

Context: Logan Roy is talking to Lukas Matsson about the possibility of selling his company to him. Logan emigrated from Scotland to America and describes what America looks like now.

ST: Now look at them, **fat as fuck, scrawny on meth** or yoga.

TT:

Category/subcategory:

Exercise 3.19

Succession SE03 EP09 – HBO

Context: Kendall Roy is having a meltdown in front of his siblings Shiv and Roman. He confesses something very serious that happened.

ST: **I killed** a kid.

TT:

Category/subcategory:

Exercise 3.20

Pulp Fiction – DVD version

Context: Vincent goes out with Marsellus' wife, Mia, for dinner.

ST: **What the fuck** is this place?

TT:

Category/subcategory:

Exercise 3.21

The White Lotus SE01 EP06 – HBO

Context: Staying at a fancy resort in Hawaii, recently married Shane Patton complains to reception because someone has defecated in his suitcase in the room where he and his wife are staying.

ST: Yeah, I'm in the Pineapple Suite, and there's **a fucking turd** in my room.

TT:

Category/subcategory:

Exercise 3.22

Once Upon a Time in Hollywood – DVD version

Context: Filmmaker Randy Miller talks to Rick Dalton about his stunt double and a wardrobe assistant.

ST: […] and, man, **she's a fucking bitch**. I just don't. Please, I…

TT:

Category/subcategory:

Exercise 3.23

Sweet Girl – Netflix

Context: Detective John Rothman is surprised after reading a note and Detective Sarah Meeker wants to know about it.

ST: -**Holy shit**! -What?

TT:

Category/subcategory:

Exercise 3.24

Knives Out – Netflix

Context: Harlan Thrombey, renowned crime novelist, is found dead and his family are being interrogated by Detective Benoit Blanc, who asks Richard Drysdale about his father.

ST: -Did he get into the party? […] -**Oh my God**!

TT:

Category/subcategory:

Exercise 3.25

Deadpool 2 – DVD version

Context: Colossus throws Deadpool from a wheelchair because the latter does not stop talking and ignores Colossus' advice.

ST: **What the fuck**!

TT:

Category/subcategory:

Exercise 3.26

Succession SE03 EP08 – HBO

Context: Gerri Kellman has some words with Roman Roy to let him know that his behaviour is far from acceptable.

ST: -I need you to stop sending me the items. […] -You don't want pictures of **my dick**. -No.

TT:

Category/subcategory:

Exercise 3.27

Deadpool 2 – DVD version

Context: Deadpool asks Colossus a question.

ST: Why can't I **fucking die**?

TT:

Category/subcategory:

Exercise 3.28

Snatch – DVD version

Context: Cousin Avi Denovitz is having an argument with Doug the Head about the way they are going to do business.

ST: -Avi! -Shut up and sit down, you **bald fuck**!

TT:

Category/subcategory:

Exercise 3.29

The Hateful Eight – DVD version

Context: In a shelter in cold Wyoming winter, O.B. Jackon and Sheriff Chris Mannix try to hammer two pieces of wood on the door to keep it from opening because of the wind. Joe Gage and Daisy Domergue yell at them to be heard because the wind is very loud.

ST: -**Goddamn it to hell**! -Gonna open if you don't…

TT:

Category/subcategory:

Exercise 3.30

Once Upon a Time in Hollywood – DVD version

Context: Stunt double Cliff Booth has a fight with a young hippy man and threatens a group of his female friends who want to approach Cliff about defending their friend.

ST: Come one step closer and **I will knock his teeth out**.

TT:

Category/subcategory:

Notes

(1) The examples have been borrowed from the STs of *Reservoir Dogs* (Quentin Tarantino, 1992), *Pulp Fiction* (Quentin Tarantino, 1994), *Inglourious Basterds* (Quentin Tarantino, 2009), *Narcos: Mexico* (Carlo Bernard and Doug Miro, 2018–2021), *Succession* (2018–, Jesse Armstrong) and *Sweet Girl* (Brian Andrew Mendoza, 2021).
(2) Retrieved from www.oxforddictionaries.com/definition/english/fanny?q=fanny.
(3) Retrieved from FOUR-LETTER WORD | meaning in the Cambridge English Dictionary.
(4) Retrieved from https://verne.elpais.com/verne/2018/12/02/articulo/1543777568 _905717.html

4 Model of Analysis for Offensive/ Taboo Language

This chapter provides readers with a methodology to follow in accordance with their different profiles and areas of interest, and is mainly aimed at future audiovisual translators, researchers and students. First, future translators who want to subtitle will be able to learn a number of translation operations in the form of strategies and techniques, given the importance of these two operations. As these translation operations are sometimes misunderstood, they will be discussed in detail. Second, I will present my own research design, aimed at researchers, so that different steps can be taken before conducting a descriptive study and model of analysis for offensive and taboo terms. Finally, a number of exercises designed to assist subtitlers and students in putting the theory into practice will be listed at the end of the chapter.

4.1 Method, Translation Strategies vs Translation Techniques

Translators need tools to deal with the difficulties imposed by the ST when it is transferred to the TT. To this aim, diverse taxonomies account for these tools in the form of translation operations. However, before delving into these concepts, we need to clarify the translation method. Hurtado Albir (1999: 32) described it as the way a translation process is carried out considering the translator's goal. The four translation methods proposed by this author are:

- Interpretative-Communicative: Translation of the sense of the ST.
- Literal: Transcodification of the ST in terms of its linguistic elements.
- Free: A modification of semiotic and communicative categories on the basis of two levels, adaptation and free version.
- Philological: Academic or critical translation.

Thus, the translator's global option will affect the TT as a whole. Once the translation method has been chosen, two types of problems can affect the translator: the difficulty of a single unit and the translator's knowledge and skills with which to deal with the problem. Translators need to find solutions to these problems. To this aim, translators make use of translation strategies and techniques. We will resort to Molina and Hurtado Albir's (2002: 507) distinction when trying to find solutions to translation problems: '[t]echniques describe the result obtained and can be used to classify different types of translation solutions. Strategies are related to the mechanisms used by translators throughout the whole translation process to find a solution to the problems they find'. Thus, as discussed by Talaván (2017), while translators use strategies to solve specific problems, the solution that materialises in the TT will determine the technique used.

4.1.1 Subtitling strategies

Different scholars have outlined various translation strategies, but one of the earliest taxonomies is that of Vinay and Darbelnet (1995 [1958]). However, considering previous studies on the subtitling of offensive and taboo language into European Spanish (Ávila-Cabrera, 2015a) and their appropriateness to this goal, I will resort to the cultural reference strategies proposed by Díaz Cintas and Remael (2021: 207–217). In addition, reformulation, a condensing operation discussed by these authors, will be considered as a subtitling strategy given its appropriateness to analyse offensive and taboo language.

(1) A loan (also named loanword) is the use of a ST term taken and used literally in the TT. This strategy is also known as 'borrowing'. An example of a loan is taken from the film *Inglourious Basterds* (Quentin Tarantino, 20007), in which the ST term *strudel*, a popular German and Austrian dessert, is subtitled in the TT literally. This is very common with drinks and food, as in the case of whisky, *paella*, etc. Technological terms are also good examples of loans from English into Spanish as in 'software', 'bluetooth', etc. Some loans from Spanish into English are *siesta* [nap], *plaza* [square], *patio* [yard], among others.

(2) Literal translation is a particular type of loan. Vinay and Darbelent (1995 [1958]) referred to it as 'word for word' or 'verbatim translation'. This strategy entails the direct transfer of the word(s) from a SL to a TL, while keeping the grammar and idiom of the original, as shown in the following example.

Reservoir Dogs – DVD version

Context: Mr Blonde remains with Officer Marvin Nash, the policeman hostage, along with Mr Orange, who bleeding to death seems to be unconscious. Officer Nash will be tortured by Mr Blonde.

ST: -**Have some fire**, scarecrow. -No, don't...

TT:
-**Ten fuego**, espantapájaros.
-¡No lo hagas!
[-**Have fire**, scarecrow.
-Do not do it!]

The ST reads 'have some fire, scarecrow', which was subtitled as *Ten fuego, espantapájaros* [Have fire, scarecrow]. We can observe how the verb phrase 'have some fire' has been literally rendered in the TT.

(3) Calque is a type of literal translation, but given the nature of its rendering, it does not sound idiomatic enough in the TT. This often happens with political or military positions. The following example introduces this strategy.

Reservoir Dogs – DVD version

Context: Nice Guy Eddie Cabot has a chat with Mr White, Mr Orange and Mr Pink while driving.

ST: He's a **wetback**. He's a friend of mine...

TT:
un **espalda mojada** amigo mío.
[a **wetback** friend of mine.]

The ST uses the insult 'wetback', an offensive term used for illegal immigrants who try to cross the Rio Grande River from Mexico to the US (Dalzell & Victor, 2008), which is subtitled into Spanish as *espalda mojada* [wetback]. This term is more common in Mexico and the US, but for the target culture in Spain, it sounds odd and the audience might miss the racist tone of this insult.

(4) Explicitation entails adding some information in the TL, which is implicit in the SL. It is the context or situation which can help the subtitler when selecting the information to be added. If we use a word with a more specific or precise meaning, we resort to specification or hyponym. By contrast, generalisation or hypernym is used when we want to utilise a word which has a broader meaning. For instance, the term 'gun' is a hyponym and 'weapon' is the hypernym. In subtitling, hypernyms are more common than hyponyms because they have an explanatory function and because of the necessity to condense the subtitle. The following example is taken from *Reservoir Dogs*.

Reservoir Dogs – DVD version

Context: In the warehouse, the rest of the gangsters get shot and Mr Orange confesses to Mr White that he is the undercover policeman. Nonetheless, Mr Pink seems to escape with the diamonds.

ST: But **I will put fucking bullets right through your heart**. You put that fucking gun down now!

TT:
pero **te voy a llenar de plomo**
si no bajas la puta pistola ya.
[but **I am going to fill you up with lead**
if you do not put down the fucking pistol now.]

We can see that the ST reads 'I will put fucking bullets right through your heart', and the TT is subtitled as *te voy a llenar de plomo* [I am going to fill you up with lead], a generalisation or hypernym, which leads to the use of fewer characters in the subtitle. A third case would be to add extra information. This could happen in the case of historical references, with which the audience might not be familiar.

(5) Substitution is another type of explicitation. Díaz Cintas and Remael (2021) regarded it as a cultural reference strategy which consists of replacing a cultural reference, which is well known in the source culture, with a similar reference in the target culture, or an expression which does not have a connection with the SL term, but with the context. In the case of insults, substitution works very well given the linguistic differences present between various languages. Let us discuss the following example with the insult 'fucker'.

Once Upon a Time in Hollywood – DVD version

Context: Rick Dalton jokes with stunt double Cliff Booth when the latter asks him to give him back his sunglasses.

ST: Oh, come get them, **fucker**. Come.

TT:
Ven a por ellas, **cabrón**.
[Come to get them, **cuckold**.]

Literally speaking, in Spanish a 'fucker' is a person who copulates, but is used with the aim of insulting. However, we can see how the ST 'fucker' was subtitled as *cabrón* [cuckold]. The insult chosen in the TT, *cabrón*, is very common in Spanish, although it really refers to a man whose wife has sex with another man, which is not normally present in the audience's minds when being heard as this offensive term is currently used in Spain as an insult whose semantic nature is not commonly known.

(6) Transposition is the substitution of a cultural reference in the source culture for another cultural reference in the target culture. This happens when the audience may not understand the reference in the ST. An example of transposition can be found in the subtitling of *Reservoir Dogs* into Spanish.

Reservoir Dogs – DVD version
Context: The film begins with eight men in black having breakfast at a café, Mr White, Mr Pink, Mr Blue, Mr Blonde, Mr Orange, Mr Brown, the big boss Joe Cabot and his son Nice Guy Eddie Cabot.
ST: I got Madonna's big dick outta my left ear, and Toby **the Jap** I-don't-know-what coming out of my right.
TT: Tengo la polla de Madonna en el oído izquierdo y… [I have the dick of Madonna in the left ear and…] a **la chinita** Toby en el derecho. [**the little Chinese (girl)** Toby in the right.]

The term 'Jap', a derogatory term addressed to the Japanese in the US during World War II, was subtitled as *la chinita* [the little Chinese (girl)]. In Spain, it is not common to refer to the Japanese derogatorily. However, it is more common when referring to the Chinese. This transposition facilitates the racist reference present in the subtitle to the Spanish audience.

(7) Lexical recreation is the invention of a new term in the TL. Sometimes this can happen when a neologism has been invented in the SL. To illustrate this case, let us focus on the following example.

Mad Max: Fury Road – HBO
Context: War boys are getting their war lorry ready to obtain petrol and sing to cheer themselves up.
ST: We are war boys! […] War boys! Fukoshima **kamakrazee** war boys!
TT: ¡Soldados! ¡Soldados **kamicafres** "Fukoshima"! [Soldiers! **Kami-brutal** soldiers!]

In the ST, we can see the term 'kamakrazee', which could be said to be a fusion of 'kamikaze' and 'crazy', that is, a neologism. The subtitler opted for a lexical recreation materialised in *kamicafres* [kami-brutal]. In this case, we can observe the fusion of the term *kami*, which comes from kamikaze (a suicidal pilot in Japanese), and *cafre* [brutal or savage]. Although it is not a grammatically correct term in the TL, it is perfectly understood by the target audience and even has a humorous tone.

(8) Compensation is 'making up for a translation loss in one exchange by being more creative or adding something extra in another' (Díaz Cintas & Remael, 2021: 215). Given the technical restrictions of subtitling, this strategy is very common when transferring offensive and taboo words. Some characters' exchanges are full of swear words and it is not always possible to subtitle all of them. If some

swear words or phrases cannot be subtitled, through compensation that character's particular linguistic feature can appear at a later stage in the subtitles.

Pulp Fiction – DVD version
Context: Mia, thinking she is going to inhale cocaine, takes an overdose of Vince's heroin powder. Vince tries to save her life with Lance, his drug dealer's help.
ST: -Hurry up, man! We're losing her! -My little black **fucking** medical book. It's like a textbook they give to nurses… I don't know! Stop bothering me!
TT: El libro de medicina. Es un libro de texto para enfermeras. [The book of medicine. It is a textbook for nurses.]
No lo sé. **Deja de joderme.** [I do not know it. **Stop fucking me.**]

As we can see in this example, the adjective 'fucking' is used before the noun phrase 'medical book'. The translator did not include the translation of it in the subtitle, probably due to spatial limitations. However, in the second subtitle, even though the ST did not include any offensive terms, the previous omission was transferred here via compensation, as the TT reveals *Deja de joderme* [Stop fucking me.].

(9) Omission is the deletion of words or phrases. It is used when the speakers' speech is fast, when the terms to be subtitled are not necessary to understand the gist or if the term in the TL does not exist. The omission of words can include proper nouns, vocatives, adverbs and conjunctions. When dealing with offensive and taboo words, 'fucking' is a term that is very likely to be deleted if the spatiotemporal restrictions require it.

Nine Perfect Strangers SE01 EP03 – Prime Video
Context: Nine strangers gather at a retreat in a health-and-wellness resort. Ben Chandler talks to Tony Hogburn and the latter acknowledges he needs some drug.
ST: Tony needs his **fucking** medicine.
TT: Y Toni necesita su medicación [And Tony needs his medication.]

As can be observed, the term 'fucking' has been deleted in the TT. If this strategy of deletion was highly recurrent when subtitling one character's exchanges which make ample use of swear words, this could lead to a loss of the function that these words have in the ST. Omission is also a highly recurrent strategy when censorial forces or self-censorship play a role in the subtitling process.

(10) Reformulation has the goal of rephrasing something in an attempt to reduce the ST or make the TT more easily understandable. However, because of the lack of equivalents between some languages when dealing with offensive and taboo words, reformulation can be regarded as a strategy to provide the TT with idiomatic renderings.

Succession SE02 EP10 – HBO
Context: Logan Roy is having a conversation with his son Kendall about marriage.
ST: And all the rest behave like **a pack of fucking stray dogs**. No.
TT: Y los demás son **unos putos parásitos**. [And the rest are **some fucking parasites**.]

If we observe the derogatory phrase of the ST 'fucking stray dogs' addressed to people, we can see that instead of being faithful to 'stray dogs', the subtitler has reduced it to *parásitos* [parasites], using fewer characters and causing a similar offensive effect. Other condensing operations via reformulation here are the change of 'behave' for *son* [are] as well as the omission of 'No' at the very end of the ST.

4.1.2 Subtitling techniques

As previously explained, once the translator has dealt with a difficulty in the translation process by making use of a strategy, it is time to observe the TT with the aim of analysing the way in which this translation operation has materialised in the TT. This is what we understand by a translation technique, that is, the visible result in the TT after having implemented a strategy (Molina & Hurtado Albir, 2002). We are going to use the taxonomy of techniques for the subtitling of offensive and taboo language elaborated by Ávila-Cabrera (2020: 129), with some slight modification. These techniques focus on the transfer and non-transfer of the load of offensive and taboo terms as shown in Table 4.1.

Table 4.1 Taxonomy of subtitling techniques for the transfer of offensive and taboo language

Translation techniques	
Transfer	• Load toned up • Load maintained • Load toned down
Non-transfer	• Load neutralised • Load omitted

There are two distinctive techniques which clearly define the transfer of this type of language. When the load of offensive and taboo language has been materialised in the TT, we can find three cases: (a) the load has been toned up or intensified with the formula chosen, perhaps because it was the subtitler's choice or because as already discussed (Section 4.1.1), the strategy of compensation can lead to the toning up of an exchange which had no offensive or taboo load at all. This is done when there has been a previous loss because of spatiotemporal constraints; (b) the load has been maintained either because the solution found has the same degree of offensiveness or a similar taboo load or because the formula chosen makes up for the load of the ST in different terms, but preserves the strength on equal terms; (c) the load has been toned down. Even though the TT has been softened, we can observe some effort made by the subtitler to transfer the load of that/those term(s). Below, I will discuss a number of cases of transfer of the offensive and taboo load.

4.1.2.1 Transfer of the load

When the transfer of the offensive or taboo load is materialised in the TT, we can distinguish the following cases: the load has been toned up, maintained or toned down. These cases are discussed next.

Narcos: Mexico SE03 EP02 – Netflix

Context: DEA agents enter a garage to confiscate drugs from the Cartel, but it is gone. One of the agents utters something out of anger.

ST: **Jesus Christ!**

TT:
   ¡Hostia puta!
   [Fucking host!]

Technique: Transfer (load toned up)

The taboo element 'Jesus Christ' in the TT is intensified by using another religious reference which gets intensified as *Hostia puta!* [Fucking host!]. The use of the term 'host' in Spanish is a common swear word or expletive, but because of its religious nature, it is not usually welcomed by Catholics. We could say here that the TT has been toned up when combining 'fucking' with what religious people consider the body of Christ, *hostia* [host].

Narcos: Mexico SE03 EP08 – Netflix

Context: DEA agent Walt Breslin talks to Alex Aragón about his family to express empathy.

ST: …we were **a fucked-up family**.

TT:
   nuestra familia era una mierda.
   [Our family was a shit.]

Technique: Transfer (load maintained)

In this example, we can see that the ST includes the adjective 'fucked-up'. The formula found in the TT maintains the load of the offensive term in this case with the use of a scatological-taboo term *una mierda* [a shit], used derogatorily. Thus, the load of the ST materialises in the TT.

Reservoir Dogs – DVD version
Context: Mr White has taken Mr Orange to the warehouse. The latter believes that he is going to die.
ST: Fuck jail, man! … **I swear to fucking God**, man.

TT:
                       Mierda, te lo juro por Dios.
                       [Shit, I swear to God.]

Technique: Transfer (load toned down)

The blasphemy 'I swear to fucking God' can be very offensive for a Spanish audience in Spain if translated faithfully. The subtitler chose to tone down the TT by just swearing to God, which can also sound strong to religious people. This example could be a case of self-censorship because the subtitler did not dare to be fully faithful to the original because of the possible effect on the audience. However, the subtitler included the term *Mierda* [Shit] to transfer the verb in the ST 'fuck' and then a swearing to God, milder but still with taboo connotations.

4.1.2.2 Non-transfer of the load

By contrast, when the load of the offensive or taboo word or expression is not materialised in the TT, we can say that the technique used is that of non-transfer. Two cases are identified: (a) the solution found neutralises the load of the ST giving place to a lack of offensiveness or taboo effect; and (b) the load of the term(s) is deleted through omission. The following two examples illustrate both cases.

Reservoir Dogs – DVD version
Context: Via flashback, Joe Cabot and his son, Nice Guy Eddie Cabot, meet Mr Blonde and Vic Vega, and then have a chat in Joe's office.
ST: Enough of **this shit**! Break it up!

TT:
                       ¡Bueno, basta!
               No estamos aquí para jugar.
                   [Good, enough!
               We are not here to play.]

Technique: Non-transfer (load neutralised)

In this example, our focus is on the word 'shit', which has been substituted by a neutral expression, *basta* [enough], so the subtitle has been neutralised probably in order to use fewer characters. Accordingly, the load of the ST term has not been transferred to the subtitle.

Reservoir Dogs – DVD version	
Context: Nice Guy Eddie Cabot has a chat with Mr White, Mr Orange and Mr Pink while driving.	
ST: What **a white bitch** will put up with, **a black bitch** wouldn't put up with for a minute.	
TT:	Una blanca aguanta cosas que una negra no. [A white bears things that a black does not.]
Technique: Non-transfer (load omitted)	

The ST text deals with the insults 'white bitch' and 'black bitch'. The subtitler, nonetheless, opted for the renderings *una blanca* [a white] and *una negra* [a black]. The omissions of 'bitch' in both cases, probably because of spatiotemporal constraints, have not allowed for the transfer of the load of these insults in the TT.

All in all, the discussion of the subtitling techniques for the treatment of offensive and taboo word(s) in subtitling is of great importance in deciphering the (non-)transfer of offensive and/or taboo load present in the original.

4.2 Research Design

This section allows readers, especially scholars and students, to establish a research design with the aim of carrying out some descriptive study in this area of language. When one wants to conduct research on some phenomenon, the first thing to consider is establishing a design. In the words of Robson (2011: 70), 'design is concerned with turning research questions into projects'. The way the research will be conducted will depend on the research questions that we want to address. The framework for research design consists of five main components: purpose(s), conceptual framework, research questions, methods and sampling procedures. All of these components (Robson, 2011: 72) are described below with the aim of establishing the main procedures to conduct research.

- Purpose(s). What is the goal of this study? Is the goal to describe, explain or understand a particular subject? Does it entail addressing a particular problem, the solution of which must be found? What will the overall effect be once the results are brought to light?
- Conceptual framework. This component concerns the theoretical premises of the object of study. Other areas to be considered are the features and aspects that characterise the object of study, which also include the interconnecting relationships of these features.
- Research questions. This component is crucial to understand the object of study. What questions is the research aiming to answer? What is it required to know in order to meet the goals of the study?

What is feasible to ask based on the resources and the time available for this research?
- Methods. What techniques of data collection will be utilised (e.g. questionnaires, interviews and participant observation)? How will the data be explored? How will we show that the data have provided us with reliable information?
- Sampling procedures. What sources will we use to obtain the data? Where and when? How will we justify the selectiveness of the necessary data to be collected?

The aforementioned components are interrelated. Starting from the purpose(s) and then moving on to the conceptual framework will allow us to define the research questions. Then, these previous components will be helpful in elaborating the other components. After establishing the research questions, we will have to choose the techniques for data collection and how the sampling procedures will be carried out. As already inferred, all these steps are paramount in order to conduct coherently designed research. Let us address all these components in detail.

4.2.1 Purpose(s)

From a descriptive approach based on the DTS (Toury, 2012) paradigm, which focuses on the way a translation is done, but does not prescribe the way it should be done, the purpose could be to explore the transfer of offensive and taboo language into European Spanish or any other language under analysis. In order to do so, we could conduct the research on a single or a few films, which would represent a case study, or a number of episodes from a TV series. In bigger studies, the focus could be on a few films by the same director or different films from different periods in the history of cinema which belong to the same genre in an attempt to observe the evolution or not of the treatment of this type of language. In addition, it would be interesting to observe whether or not in the case of multilingual films if the secondary languages were translated via a pivot text, which is usually in English, before transferring all the ST in different languages into the TT (Díaz Cintas & Remael, 2021). This is an important aspect because 'pivot translations can linguistically determine the TT, as far as multilingual films are concerned' (Ávila-Cabrera, 2013: 99).

In general terms, the purpose of the study could be to ascertain whether the load of the offensive or taboo term or phrase is transferred to the TT or, by contrast, to explore if the non-transfer of the load is due to cases of (ideological) manipulation or (self-)censorship, or because of the technical restrictions of subtitling. For the latter, a subtitling software program should be used. It would be necessary to pay attention to the subtitle settings of the audiovisual programme under study to observe the characters permitted in each of the subtitles and their duration.

4.2.2 Conceptual framework

The representation of the different elements to be considered in a research study will be defined here to determine their properties and the way they interact with each other. In the words of Maxwell (2005: 33), 'the system of concepts, assumptions, expectations, beliefs, and theories that supports and informs' some research are items of importance in the design. Figure 4.1, based on Ávila-Cabrera (2014: 112) with slight modifications, depicts the layers that define the conceptual framework (Robson, 2011) dealt with in the following proposal for a research design.

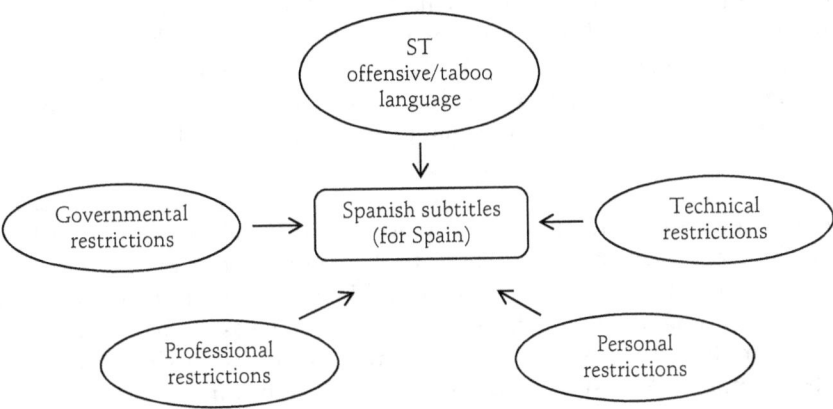

Figure 4.1 Example of conceptual framework

Figure 4.1 shows the concepts of interest in the process of subtitling offensive and taboo language into Spanish. Several restrictions such as governmental, professional, personal and technical (Díaz Cintas, 2001b) can be observed, which I will discuss next.

First, governmental restrictions are common under dictatorships, such as those already presented (Section 2.6.3) in Spain, Italy, Greece, Portugal and Germany during the 20th century. Today in Spain, the subtitling of current audiovisual programmes or films is free of this type of restriction, but it must not be ignored with other types of research which date back to previous decades. Second, professional restrictions concern those imposed by the client's preferences with regard to the way the product must be subtitled. It is well known that during children's screen time many words are forbidden, which are written on a black list, as is the case with Disney and other production companies (Talaván et al., 2016). In fact, there are subtitling versions for flights, which consider the potential viewing of films or TV series by children, as we can see in Figure 4.2.

Tomb Raider – Delta Airlines version
Context: After some adventure, Lara Croft, beaten and bruised, talks to Lu Ren.
ST: At least we're not dead yet. No, **shit**!
TT: At least we're not dead yet. No, sugar.

Figure 4.2 Example of manipulation in film subtitles for flight versions

As we can see from the above example, both the ST and TT are in English, that is, these are intralingual subtitles. The ST includes the term 'shit', which an English native speaker would understand. However, the subtitle in the English version substitutes that term for the euphemism 'sugar', manipulating the subtitle. To conclude this point, clients can be production companies, film distributors and TV channels which, in the case of offensive and taboo exchanges, can impose milder or stronger restrictions in accordance with several factors.

Third, as discussed when dealing with manipulation (Section 2.6), sometimes translators impose restrictions on themselves when subtitling certain terms, which Díaz Cintas (2012) referred to as cases of self-censorship or ideological manipulation. This is a very sensitive process when subtitling blasphemy into Spanish, in which case some other offensive formulas rather than a direct insult to 'God' or 'Jesus Christ' are usually the norm (Ávila-Cabrera, 2020). Fourth, subtitling is characterised by its technical restrictions in the form of spatiotemporal constraints (Section 2.2.1). Given the restrictions of this AVT mode, Díaz Cintas (2012) discussed technical manipulation because of the condensing of the ST which needs to occur during its transfer to the subtitles. In this particular case, offensive and taboo exchanges are prone to being reduced or even deleted when space limitations require it.

We can see up to four different restrictions in Figure 4.1. When they negatively affect the final product or subtitles, the result can be an unfaithful TT which diverges from the original script. Not being able to transfer the speakers' linguistic features in the subtitles can lead to the loss of the ST thematic function, making the audience miss relevant linguistic and semantic features or having a negative impact on their viewing. Nonetheless, it would be naïve to think that a subtitling process is free of all restrictions. As already discussed, subtitling is very much characterised by the condensing of the original. It is my goal to make readers consider the conceptual framework presented here as a model that can be adapted to their own needs when conducting research on the treatment of offensive and taboo language in subtitling from English into Spanish, or with any other linguistic combinations.

4.2.3 Research questions

Once the purpose and the conceptual framework of a study have been defined, finding the best research questions for our goals is paramount to having a well-structured research design. Let us think of some general questions which might be of interest in accordance with the goals of this book.

(1) What are the most recurrent offensive and taboo subcategories encountered in the corpus under analysis? In order to address this question, a descriptive analysis should be carried out. To that aim, the researcher should go through all the instances of offensive and taboo language in the ST and check on their transfer in the TT in the form of the subtitles analysed. The answer to this question would allow us to know if there were more offensive or taboo words or expressions in the ST. Additionally, another question could be established in terms of knowing whether the offensive words or phrases were subtitled as offensive or not. The same would apply to taboo words or phrases. This could be an interesting study given that languages have their own systems when swearing, insulting, dealing with taboo topics, etc.

(2) What are the most recurrent translation strategies used during the subtitling process? The answer to this question would permit us to know the translation operations carried out by the translator or subtitler. From a DTS approach, the current tendency is to explore the way the translation was done, without prescribing how it should have been done.

(3) What are the most recurrent translation techniques used during the subtitling process? The answer to this question is of great importance in the context of the book. When we observe the effect that the transfer of offensive and taboo terms has on the TT, we then want to find out whether or not the load of these terms has materialised in the subtitles. To this aim, the techniques used will clarify if there has been transfer or non-transfer of the load of offensive and taboo terms.

(4) Was the transfer of offensive and taboo language faithful to the original? This question is a continuation of the previous and one that is of paramount importance. In order to address it, the techniques used during the translation process will shed light on the answer. When the offensive and taboo load in the subtitle is toned down, maintained or toned up, we say that the transfer has occurred. By contrast, when the load in the TT is neutralised or omitted, we have a non-transfer case; in other words, the TT is not totally faithful to the original.

(5) Were the cases of non-transfer of the offensive and taboo load justified because of the spatiotemporal constraints in subtitling? The answer to this question is not an easy one because it requires us to make use of some professional or freeware subtitle editors in order to know the duration of each subtitle as well as the number of characters allowed. When the answer to this question is affirmative, the implementation of the operations that neutralise or omit the load of the offensive and taboo words or phrases is legitimate. On the other hand, if researchers do not have access to the audiovisual material using a subtitling program, they can only conduct the analysis from a linguistic point of view.

(6) Were the secondary languages of the multilingual corpus translated via a pivot text? This question exclusively applies to the analysis of multilingual films – a normal practice in the AVT market. For example, the film *Inglourious Basterds* (Quentin Tarantino, 2009) is multilingual. Its main language is English, and its secondary languages are German, French and Italian. In an interview with the subtitler into Spanish, Arturo Enríquez, he confirmed that these secondary languages had previously been translated into a pivot text in English (Ávila-Cabrera, 2016a). In the case of translations through a pivot text, some lexical and semantic features can be lost.

There may be more research questions which align well with the purposes of the study. Our aim here is to offer a number of them which revolve around the transfer of the load of this type of language, which in many cases can be a real challenge to subtitlers because of all the aspects discussed so far in this book.

4.2.4 Methods

To begin with, the focus of this study is on the translation operations during the subtitling process and exploring its effects in the TT. In the case of a study looking into a film or some episodes or a season of a TV series, that is, a small corpus, we would resort to the case study method. As Robson (2011: 522) put it, a case study is 'a research design focusing on the study of single cases or a small number of cases [...] case study design focuses on the case in its context, typically using multiple methods of data collection'. The main goal is to shed light on the transfer of offensive and taboo language into a TT in Spanish, for example.

With the aim of obtaining more reliable results and reducing the chances of obtaining erroneous results, researchers can make use of triangulation, which Robson (2011: 195) defined as 'a valuable and widely used strategy involving the use of multiple resources to enhance the rigour of the research'. How can we make use of triangulation? If we observe a phenomenon under study from different angles, we can say that we are triangulating data. The mixed-method research or multi-strategy research designs combine quantitative and qualitative data. Then, both approaches need to be treated independently and through observation of the results, we can corroborate or refute the soundness of the findings of our research.

Creswell (2003) referred to 'sequential explanatory design' as that in which quantitative data is collected and analysed, followed by the collection and analysis of qualitative data. Priority is given to the quantitative data and the two methods are then integrated during the interpretation stage. Let us say we have analysed the transfer of offensive and taboo language in a film, that is, a case study. The quantitative data would respond to the way in which the instances of offensive and taboo language have been subtitled in the TT. Then the qualitative data in the form of questionnaires and interviews could be obtained from subtitlers, who should have answered questions relating to the way they subtitled the type of language under study.

4.2.5 Sampling procedures

The sources from which the data have been collated as well as the steps followed for their analysis respond to the sampling procedures. In the first place, the researcher who wants to analyse a film or TV series, for example, should choose whether the audiovisual content appears in a VHS, a DVD, Blu-ray or a digital platform. The information collected here would account for the quantitative data. Then, if it were possible and feasible, a qualitative data collection method, such as an interview or questionnaire, needs to be chosen. The analysis of the interviews, questionnaires, for example, would allow for the corroboration or refutation of the results obtained from the analysis of the subtitles. It is not always possible to make use of triangulation, for which reason many studies based on the DTS paradigm resort to quantitative data.

4.3 Exercises

Subtitle the following dialogue exchanges into Spanish carrying out proper segmentation. Then, think about the category and subcategory of offensive and taboo language in the ST, written in bold type. Next, think of the possible translation strategies and techniques used during the translation operations and specify if the translation load has been transferred (toned up, maintained or toned down) or not transferred (neutralised or omitted).

Note: In real practice, the whole ST should be available to the subtitler because this professional practice entails taking into account both the complete ST and the information provided by the audio and visual channel. However, the exercises presented here are aimed at practising possible renderings of some challenging expressions which have offensive and/or taboo words.

Exercise 4.1

Narcos: Mexico SE03 EP05 – Netflix

Context: DEA agent Walt Breslin talks to his superior James Kuykendall.

ST: With all due respect, Sir, I'm here **to get shit done**.

TT:

Category/subcategory:
Strategy/technique:

Exercise 4.2

Succession SE03 EP08 – HBO

Context: Stewy Hosseini and Sandi Furness meet Logan Roy, Roman Roy and Tom Wambsgans at an office in their company building to discuss some business.

ST: Great. We're all over the **fucking** moon. What is this?

TT:

Category/subcategory:
Strategy/technique:

Exercise 4.3

Deadpool 2 – DVD version

Context: Deadpool talks to a group of Japanese gangs with whom he is fighting.

ST: I don't bargain, **pumpkin fucker**.

TT:

Category/subcategory:
Strategy/technique:

Exercise 4.4

Succession SE03 EP08 – HBO

Context: Stewy Hosseini and Sandi Furness meet Logan Roy, Roman Roy and Tom Wambsgans at an office in their company building to discuss some business.

ST: -Matsson's a visionary. -Sure. Because **he's tripping balls**.

TT:

Category/subcategory:
Strategy/technique:

Exercise 4.5

Succession SE03 EP08 – HBO

Context: Logan Roy meets his son Kendall over dinner and they have a serious conversation about Kendall's addictions.

ST: ...and whenever you **fucked up,** I cleaned up **your shit**.

TT:

Category/subcategory:
Strategy/technique:

Category/subcategory:
Strategy/technique:

Exercise 4.6

Deadpool 2 – DVD version

Context: Deadpool has a conversation with his wife Vanessa and asks her a question.

ST: I don't know what this is.

TT:

Category/subcategory:
Strategy/technique:

Exercise 4.7

Snatch – DVD version

Context: Mickey O'Neil is fighting Gorgeous George in a stable. Mickey tells Gorgeous George the following before knocking him down.

ST: **Deadly kick** for a **fat fucker,** you know that?

TT:

Category/subcategory:
Strategy/technique:

Category/subcategory:
Strategy/technique:

Exercise 4.8

Succession SE03 EP08 – HBO

Context: The Roy siblings are in Italy for their mother's wedding. Also present is their father and CEO of the firm, Logan Roy. Roman is talking to Shiv, Tom and Gerri about business.

ST: Yeah, my goodness, gummy love bite from the **fucking** toddlers.

TT:

Category/subcategory:
Strategy/technique:

Exercise 4.9

Knives Out – Netflix

Context: Harlan Thrombey, renowned crime novelist, is found dead and his family are being interrogated by Detective Benoit Blanc. Marta Cabrera is talking to Benoit and Meg Thrombey mutters.

ST: No, it's not okay. **What the hell!**

TT:

Category/subcategory:
Strategy/technique:

Exercise 4.10

Knives Out – Netflix

Context: Harlan Thrombey, renowned crime novelist, is found dead and his family are being interrogated by Detective Benoit Blanc. Linda Drysdale addresses Marta Cabrera insulting her.

ST: Oh you **little bitch**!

TT:

Category/subcategory:
Strategy/technique:

Exercise 4.11

Knives Out – Netflix

Context: Harlan Thrombey, renowned crime novelist, is found dead and his family are being interrogated by Detective Benoit Blanc. Walt Thrombey answers Benoit's question about the night of the party.

ST: No, **Jesus**. We did not get into it.

TT:

Category/subcategory:
Strategy/technique:

Exercise 4.12

Knives Out – Netflix

Context: Harlan Thrombey, renowned crime novelist, is found dead and his family are being interrogated by Detective Benoit Blanc. Ransom Drysdale addresses Detective Benoit Blanc disrespectfully after feeling threatened by the detective's words.

ST: Shut up with **that Kentucky-fried, Foghorn Leghorn drawl**!

TT:

Category/subcategory:
Strategy/technique:

Exercise 4.13

Narcos: Mexico SE03 EP01 – Netflix

Context: DEA agent Walt Breslin tries to calm Mike down after revealing to him that he is an undercover agent.

ST: I need you to **shut the fuck up** and calm down.

TT:

Category/subcategory:
Strategy/technique:

Exercise 4.14

Deadpool 2 – DVD version

Context: Colossus has grabbed Deadpool by the neck because he does not pay enough attention to him. Deadpool complains after being released.

ST: Oh, **Jesus Christ**!

TT:

Category/subcategory:
Strategy/technique:

Exercise 4.15

Deadpool 2 – DVD version

Context: Deadpool is being given a ride by Dopinder, a taxi driver. The former asks the latter a question.

ST: What's your poison? A little, uh, **cokey, cokey**.

TT:

Category/subcategory:
Strategy/technique:

Exercise 4.16

Reservoir Dogs – DVD version

Context: The film begins with eight men in black having breakfast at a café, Mr White, Mr Pink, Mr Blue, Mr Blonde, Mr Orange, Mr Brown, the big boss Joe Cabot and his son Nice Guy Eddie Cabot.

ST: Never mind what you normally would do.

TT:

Category/subcategory:
Strategy/technique:

Exercise 4.17

Knives Out – Netflix

Context: Harlan Thrombey, renowned crime novelist, is found dead and his family are being interrogated by Detective Benoit Blanc. He talks to all the family defending Marta Cabrera over their accusations towards their father's death.

ST: You have all treated her **like shit** to steal back a fortune that you lost and she deserves.
TT:

Category/subcategory:
Strategy/technique:

Exercise 4.18

Deadpool 2 – DVD version

Context: Deadpool is moaning to Blind Al, who tries to cheer him up.

ST: It's a little hard to hear you with that **pity dick in your mouth.**
TT:

Category/subcategory:
Strategy/technique:

Exercise 4.19

Pulp Fiction – DVD version

Context: Mia, thinking she is going to inhale cocaine, takes an overdose of Vince's heroin powder. Vince tries to save her life with Lance, his drug dealer's help.

ST: Oh, **Jesus fucking Christ!**
TT:

Category/subcategory:
Strategy/technique:

Exercise 4.20

Succession SE03 EP08 – HBO

Context: Shiv and her brother Roman are having a conversation on a private jet. He proposes some idea regarding her mother's soon-to-be wedding which she rejects.

ST: **Fuck it.**
TT:

Category/subcategory:
Strategy/technique:

Exercise 4.21

Deadpool 2 – DVD version

Context: Deadpool has a conversation with barman Weasel at the bar.

ST: And nobody **fucking** realizes it.

TT:

Category/subcategory:
Strategy/technique:

Exercise 4.22

Once Upon a Time in Hollywood – DVD version

Context: Filmmaker Randy Miller tells stunt double Cliff Booth to get dressed for some film shooting.

ST: Okay, you **fucking horse's ass**. Let's get you over to wardrobe.

TT:

Category/subcategory:
Strategy/technique:

Exercise 4.23

Deadpool 2 – DVD version

Context: The film begins with Deadpool committing suicide by blowing himself to pieces. While flying through the air, he says some words to Wolverine.

ST: Fuck Wolverine. [...] Then **the hairy motherfucker** ups the ante by dying.

TT:

Category/subcategory:
Strategy/technique:

Exercise 4.24

Once Upon a Time in Hollywood – DVD version

Context: Pussycat, a young hippy girl, is on the street and insults a police officer when she sees him in a car.

ST: **Fuck you**, you **fucking pig**.

TT:

Category/subcategory:
Strategy/technique:

Category/subcategory:
Strategy/technique:

Exercise 4.25

Knives Out – Netflix

Context: Harlan Thrombey, renowned crime novelist, is found dead. When his family is told that Marta Cabrera is inheriting Harlan Thrombey's fortune, grandson Jacob Thrombey insults her.

ST: You **had sex** with my grandpa, you **dirty anchor baby**?

TT:

Category/subcategory:
Strategy/technique:

Category/subcategory:
Strategy/technique:

Exercise 4.26

Snatch – DVD version

Context: Turco and Tommy are trying to do business with Micky, the leader of a family of gypsies, and is offered a caravan with no wheels as part of their deal.

ST: Why **the fuck** do I want a caravan that's got no **fucking** wheels?

TT:

Category/subcategory:
Strategy/technique:

Category/subcategory:
Strategy/technique:

Exercise 4.27

Deadpool 2 – DVD version

Context: A criminal asks for help as Deadpool is preparing to kill him.

ST: Hurry up and open this **fucking** door, and let's kill this **motherfucker**.

TT:

Category/subcategory:
Strategy/technique:

Category/subcategory:
Strategy/technique:

Exercise 4.28

Pulp Fiction – DVD version

Context: Mia, thinking she is going to inhale cocaine, takes an overdose of Vince's heroin powder. Vince tries to save her life with Lance, his drug dealer's help.

ST: What **the hell** was that?

TT:

Category/subcategory:
Strategy/technique:

Exercise 4.29

Deadpool 2 – DVD version

Context: Firefist talks to Deadpool on the street damaged by the fire the former has made. After Firefist throws Colossus away with a fire ball, Deadpool reacts.

ST: Oh, **shit**! That **fucking** does it!

TT:

Category/subcategory:
Strategy/technique:

Category/subcategory:
Strategy/technique:

Exercise 4.30

Snatch – DVD version

Context: Bullet-Tooth Tony is being held at gunpoint by Sol and his pals. Bullet-Tooth-Tony challenges them with his daring words.

ST: There are two types of **balls**: there are **big brave balls**, and there are **little faggot balls**.

TT:

Category/subcategory:
Strategy/technique:

Category/subcategory:
Strategy/technique:

Category/subcategory:
Strategy/technique:

Exercise 4.31

Once Upon a Time in Hollywood – DVD version

Context: Rick Dalton is in his wagon and does not stop swearing and talking to himself because of his bad acting performance.

ST: You're **a fucking miserable drunk**.

TT:

Category/subcategory:
Strategy/technique:

Exercise 4.32

Deadpool 2 – DVD version

Context: Firefist has damaged the street with fire and is surrounded by the police. He challenges everyone looking at him.

ST: Do you wanna **fucking die**?

TT:

Category/subcategory:
Strategy/technique:

Exercise 4.33

Nine Perfect Strangers SE01 EP04 – Prime Video

Context: Nine strangers gather at a retreat in a health-and-wellness resort. Masha Dmitrichenko, the guru, tells the group they have been micro dosing them with a drug, psilocybin. Tony Hogburn complains to her after hearing it.

ST: **God**, you got **some balls** shaming me about some wine and a couple of Kit Kats. All the while, **you're dosing us with psychedelics**?

TT:

Category/subcategory:
Strategy/technique:

Category/subcategory:
Strategy/technique:

Category/subcategory:
Strategy/technique:

Exercise 4.34

Django Unchained – Netflix

Context: Django shoots Stephen in the kneecap and the latter insults him.

ST: Oh, sweet Jesus, let me **kill** this **"n****r"**.

TT:

Category/subcategory:
Strategy/technique:

Category/subcategory:
Strategy/technique:

Exercise 4.35

Knives Out – Netflix

Context: Harlan Thrombey, renowned crime novelist, is found dead. When his family is told that Marta Cabrera is inheriting Harlan Thrombey's fortune, Linda Drysdale starts asking Marta disrespectful questions in anger.

ST: What were you doing? **Were you boinking** my father?

TT:

Category/subcategory:
Strategy/technique:

Exercise 4.36

Once Upon a Time in Hollywood – DVD version

Context: Rick Dalton is in his wagon and does not stop swearing and talking to himself because of his bad acting performance.

ST: **Fucking damn it**, Rick, **I swear to God**. Forgot your **fucking** lines,

TT:

Category/subcategory:
Strategy/technique:

Category/subcategory:
Strategy/technique:

Category/subcategory:
Strategy/technique:

Exercise 4.37

Nine Perfect Strangers SE01 EP07 – Prime Video

Context: Nine strangers gather at a retreat in a health-and-wellness resort. Masha Dmitrichenko has a conversation with Carmel Schneider and the latter starts talking to her aggressively.

ST: My daughters. You **fucking bitch**, they're my daughters, Lillian! **I fucking hate you.**

TT:

Category/subcategory:
Strategy/technique:

Category/subcategory:
Strategy/technique:

Exercise 4.38

Fleabag SE01 EP01– Prime Video

Context: Fleabag is having sex with her hookup Arsehole Guy, while narrating to the audience what is to come.

ST: After some pretty standard **bouncing**, you realise **he's edging towards your asshole**.

TT:

Category/subcategory:
Strategy/technique:

Category/subcategory:
Strategy/technique:

Exercise 4.39

Nine Perfect Strangers SE01 EP01 – Prime Video

Context: Nine strangers gather at a retreat in a health-and-wellness resort. Frances Welty receives a phone call with bad news, so she starts releasing her anger by talking to herself.

ST: Dead to the **fucking** world.

TT:

Category/subcategory:
Strategy/technique:

Category/subcategory:
Strategy/technique:

Exercise 4.40

Fleabag SE02 EP05 – Prime Video

Context: Fleabag is in her shop. Her ex brother-in-law, Martin, pays her a visit. They start arguing and then move on to insulting each other.

ST: -**I will take you down, fucker.** -I will take you down, fucker. -No. -**Fuck you!** -Fuck you!

TT:

Category/subcategory:
Strategy/technique:

Category/subcategory:
Strategy/technique:

Category/subcategory:
Strategy/technique:

Answer Key

Chapter 2

The following examples are taken from official subtitles on DVDs and digital platforms. They are not aimed at prescribing the way the subtitles should have been made. Instead, they offer a possible solution to the exercise. You will find the context of the scene, the original script or ST along with the TT in the form of the Spanish subtitle. Below, you will find a back translation, which although it may not sound idiomatic enough, its purpose is to make the reader see the way the foreign language text is structured, in this case Spanish. Also, pay attention to the segmentation or line break of the subtitle in order to learn how to divide the lines. After the solution, presented as a subtitle, the reader will find some discussion on the translation/subtitling operations carried out for text reduction (Roales Ruiz, 2017). These subtitles do not present the reading speed, their duration or the number of characters allowed. Instead, they are aimed as a point of departure to be able to find solutions from a linguistic point of view.

Exercise 2.1

Reservoir Dogs – DVD version

Context: The film begins with eight men in black having breakfast at a café, Mr White, Mr Pink, Mr Blue, Mr Blonde, Mr Orange, Mr Brown, the big boss Joe Cabot and his son Nice Guy Eddie Cabot.

ST: Oh, yeah, man. It's fucking great… You know what I heard the other day?

TT:
Está de puta madre.
¿Sabes lo que oí el otro día?
[It is of whore mother (fucking cool).
Do you know what I heard the other day?]

The subtitler has opted for a two-liner. 'Oh, yeah, man' in the ST has been omitted to save characters, considered a total reduction strategy. Also, as Spanish allows for the omission of the subject, not translating 'you' has also saved at least three characters, another strategy for total reduction.

Exercise 2.2

Reservoir Dogs – DVD version

Context: The film begins with eight men in black having breakfast at a café, Mr White, Mr Pink, Mr Blue, Mr Blonde, Mr Orange, Mr Brown, the big boss Joe Cabot and his son Nice Guy Eddie Cabot.

ST: I know, motherfucker. I just heard it.

TT:
>Ya lo sé, coño.
>Acabo de oírlo.
>[I know it, fuck (bloody hell).
>I have just heard it.]

In this case, the subtitler has changed the expletive 'motherfucker' for another expletive which occupies fewer characters, *coño* [fuck (bloody hell)]. Given the variety of swear words in Spanish, the subtitler has partially reduced the ST by using a shorter term which substitutes a longer term.

Exercise 2.3

Reservoir Dogs – DVD version

Context: Mr White has taken Mr Orange to the warehouse. The latter believes that he is going to die.

ST: The situation is I'm shot in the belly. Without medical attention, I'm gonna die.

TT:
>Tengo una bala en el estómago
>y sin ayuda médica moriré.
>[I have a bullet in the stomach
>and without medical aid I will die.]

The subtitler has resorted to total reduction with the omission of 'the situation is', as it is not necessary to understand the scene. Instead of translating the passive voice 'be shot' literally, the change to the active voice in the form of the present simple *Tengo* [I have] has been used as a partial reduction strategy. Then we can observe that the conjunction *y* [and] appears in the bottom line following the segmentation conventions of the subtitling practice. Thanks to this operation, the independent sentences of the ST have been put together. 'I'm gonna die' has been translated as a future simple, reducing the number of characters and changing a complex structure to a simple one, that is, partial reduction.

Exercise 2.4

Reservoir Dogs – DVD version

Context: Mr White and Mr Orange review the steps for the jewellery robbery.

ST: If you wanna know something and he won't tell you, cut off one of his fingers. The little one.

TT:
> Si no responde a tus preguntas,
> le cortas un dedo, el meñique.
> [If he does not answer your questions,
> you cut him a finger off, the little one.]

The conditional sentence closely translated would contain too many words. Thus, the subtitler condenses the if-clause using a negative verb *Si no responde a tus preguntas* [If he does not answer your questions,], which perfectly summarises the whole conditional sentence 'If you wanna know something and he won't tell you'. Although 'wanna' has been reformulated with this partial reduction operation, if the subtitler had to translate it, it should be through a grammatically correct phrase, as subtitles must show grammatical structures. However, the characters' register can be marked with other words, such as swear words for instance.

Exercise 2.5

Pulp Fiction – DVD version

Context: In a club, Butch Coolidge, a prizefighter, meets Marsellus Wallace as they are going to prepare a boxing fight where he must be beaten by a knockout.

ST: Motherfuckers who thought their ass would age like wine.

TT:
> Hijos de puta que piensan
> que su culo envejece como el vino.
> [Sons of whore who think
> that their ass grows old like the wine.]

The partial reduction used here is not complicated to achieve, but works very well. The tenses in the past simple 'thought' and conditional simple 'would age' are translated as present simple in the subtitle, *piensan* [think] and *envejece* [grows old]. This way, the subtitler has avoided the use of extra characters.

Exercise 2.6

Pulp Fiction – DVD version

Context: Vincent is in his dealer's house to buy some heroin.

ST: And some dickless piece of shit fucked with it.

TT:
> y un hijo de puta sin huevos
> me lo jode.
> [and a son of a whore without balls
> fucks it to me.]

The phrase 'dickless piece of shit' would not work semantically in the TT if translated faithfully given that 'dickless' is an insult used in English, but not in Spanish. Thus, the subtitler has opted for a more natural rendering of this phrase as *un hijo de puta sin huevos* [a son of a whore without balls]. As for the tense, the past simple 'fucked' would have used more characters than the present simple tense employed *jode* [fucks], aiming at a partial reduction. As for the segmentation, the phrase *un hijo de puta sin huevos* has been kept undivided in the top line preserving a correct segmentation, and although the layout is not pyramidal, priority is given to segmentation rules.

Exercise 2.7

Pulp Fiction – DVD version
Context: Vincent is in his dealer's house to buy some heroin.
ST: What's more chicken-shit than fucking with a man's automobile?
TT: Joderle el coche a un tío es de cobardes. [Fucking the car to a guy is cowardly.]

The ST closely translated would entail providing the subtitle with a long question. However, the subtitler has been able to transfer the gist of it. Instead of subtitling the direct question as such, the partial reduction operation here has been: (1) to use the second clause of the question as the subject in the subtitle *Joderle el coche a un tío* [Fucking the car to a guy], making use of a statement; (2) to reformulate the question 'What's more chicken-shit' used in the phrase *es de cobardes* [is cowardly], in this way saving a considerable number of characters. Albeit the ST includes the terms 'chicken-shit' and 'fucking', we can observe that the subtitler has kept the load in the form of *Joderle* [fuck], not being able to include two offensive terms for the sake of space.

Exercise 2.8

Pulp Fiction – DVD version
Context: Vincent goes out with Marsellus' wife, Mia, for dinner.
ST: Another way would be he was thrown out by Marsellus.
TT: Otra forma sería que Marsellus le tiró por la ventana. [Another way would be that Marsellus threw him out of the window.]

This is another example in which the passive voice 'he was thrown' is changed to the active voice *Marsellus le tiró* [Marsellus threw him], that is, a partial reduction strategy. We must clarify that while the passive voice is very common in English, the Spanish language uses more impersonal sentences with *se* [it is] or the active voice. This change of passive voice to active is very recurrent in the subtitling into Spanish because of the character reduction that it entails.

Exercise 2.9

Pulp Fiction – DVD version

Context: Mia, thinking she is going to inhale cocaine, takes an overdose of Vince's heroin powder. Vince tries to save her life with Lance, his drug dealer's help.

ST: I thought you told those fucking assholes never to call here this late!

TT:
>Creí que les habías dicho
>que no llamaran tan tarde.
>[I thought you had told them
>not to call so late.]

In this example, the insult 'fucking assholes' has been omitted in the subtitle, resorting to total reduction. Are we dealing with a self-censorship case? Probably not. We have seen in previous examples that *Pulp Fiction* is full of offensive and taboo terms. The subtitler might have to omit elements in favour of abiding by the technical restrictions and sometimes insults need to be omitted in favour of transmitting the gist of the ST. This is even more recurrent when the viewer is used to seeing characters swearing much of the time. In addition, 'here' is also omitted in the subtitle considering that the spectator can see through the visual channel that 'here' is the place where they are.

Exercise 2.10

Pulp Fiction – DVD version

Context: By chance, Butch comes across Marsellus in the street. After Butch runs him over, Marsellus goes after him and they enter a shop. Butch starts punching Marsellus, but then both of them are kidnapped in an attempt to be raped. In the end, Butch releases Marsellus from the rapists and the latter lets him go with the condition of leaving LA.

ST: Now you just wait a goddamn minute, now! What the fuck you up to?

TT:
>Eh, espere un minuto.
>¿Qué coño cree que hace?
>[Ah, wait for a minute.
>What the fuck do you think that you are doing?]

There are two offensive words in the ST: 'goddamn' and 'What the fuck'. To be able to use fewer characters in the subtitle, the subtitler has opted for omitting the former, by means of total reduction, and keeping the latter, *Qué coño* [What the fuck]. The time expression 'now', which is repeated in the ST, has been changed to a single *Eh* [Ah], in the first place and omitted in the second, making use of partial and total reduction, respectively. The use of *usted* – a polite formula for 'you' in Spanish that is used with people who we do not know and to show respect – is visible in the two verbs *espere* [wait] and *hace* [you do]. We could infer that they have been used to save characters, but this seems to respond to the conversation on the screen among individuals who do not know each other well.

Exercise 2.11

Pulp Fiction – DVD version
Context: After Jules and Vincent have killed most of the youngsters and retrieved Marsellus' suitcase, Vincent accidentally shoots one of the youngsters in the face while driving and their car remains full of blood and brains.
ST: It means that's it for me. From here on in, you can consider my ass retired.
TT: Para mí se acabó. Desde ahora considérame retirado. [For me it is over. From now consider me retired.]

The way 'to say something is over' is shorter in the TT than in the ST in the form of *Para mí se acabó* [For me it is over]. Thus, total reduction has been implemented with the omission of 'It means'. Next, using the word 'ass' to refer to a person is common in slang. The subtitler has opted, nonetheless, for a partial reduction with the use of an object pronoun to refer to himself, *considérame* [consider me]. We can therefore see how this long ST has been transferred by using fewer characters in the TT.

Exercise 2.12

Pulp Fiction – DVD version
Context: Jules and Vincent are at Jimmie's house where they will have to clean the car and get rid of the dead body. Winston, the Wolf, will help them do so before Jimmie's wife gets back home from work.
ST: I don't give a damn if he does.
TT: Me la trae floja. [I do not give a damn.]

The ST has a conditional sentence, but the subordinate clause 'if he does' has been omitted on the basis of total reduction. The main clause has been the one subtitled, but changing the negative verb for an affirmative verb, resorting to partial reduction. Thus, the subtitler has used fewer characters with the solution employed, *Me la trae floja* [I do not give a damn]. This expression can be considered a euphemistic formula which comes from *Me suda la polla* [It sweats the dick], used when a male wants to express that he is not interested in something or someone.

Exercise 2.13

Inglourious Basterds – DVD version

Context: American Lieutenant Aldo Raine (Lt Raine) addresses his newly formed eight-man Jewish-American commando unit, known by the Germans as the Basterds.

ST: That's why any and every son of a bitch we find wearing a Nazi uniform... they're gonna die.

TT:
Por eso todo hijoputa
que veamos con uniforme nazi
[That is why every son of a whore
we see in a Nazi uniform]

va a morir.
[is going to die.]

This ST has been transferred through two subtitles. In the case of the former, 'any and every' has been condensed as *todo* [every], omitting the first elements in the phrase. In addition, we can see how 'son of a bitch' has been subtitled as *hijoputa* [son of bitch]. Even though this term is accepted grammatically, it is not common in written language but can be understood by the target audience. The effect is quite natural and avoids the use of extra characters as in the case of *hijo de puta* [son of the bitch]. As for the second subtitle, we can assume that spatiotemporal restrictions did not allow the subtitler to include more terms in the TT. Then, the subject which is included in the first subtitle 'any and every son of a bitch' is not needed in the second one. It is a case of total reduction because the Spanish language can omit the subjects when necessary, allowing for the subtitler to use fewer characters.

Exercise 2.14

Inglourious Basterds – DVD version

Context: Via flashback, the narrator describes sergeant Hugo Stiglitz, who killed 13 Gestapo officers when he was a German private. The way he joined the Basterds is then shown.

ST: We know there's another Kraut patrol fucking around here somewhere.

TT:
Sabemos que hay
otra patrulla boche jodiendo por ahí.
[We know that there is
another rascal patrol fucking over there.]

The term *Kraut* has been used since World War II as a racial insult to the Germans. A literal rendering of this term could have been cryptic to the target audience, which would probably have required further characters to be understood. The subtitler might have decided to use the term *boche*, a slang term for 'rascal', used by the French to refer to the Germans during World War I.[1] Also, instead of translating 'here somewhere', the latter element has been omitted in the subtitle, translating only *ahí* [there].

Exercise 2.15

Inglourious Basterds – DVD version

Context: Lt Raine attempts to intimidate sergeant Rachtmann since he does not give the German patrol away. As the German sergeant refuses to inform the Basterds, he is finally killed by the Bear Jew.

ST: About now I'd be shitting my pants if I was you.

TT:
En vuestro lugar, me estaría cagando.
[In your place, I would be shitting.]

First, 'About now' has been treated with total reduction through its omission in the subtitle as it is deemed unnecessary. The if-clause 'if I was you', grammatically incorrect, has been placed at the beginning of the subtitle, being reformulated as *En vuestro lugar* [In your place]. Then, the scatological verb has been transferred in the subtitle as *me estaría cagando* [I would be shitting], but 'my pants' has been omitted, resorting to total reduction. It is not necessary to include this phrase in the TT as the verb in the TL is very descriptive and one does not need to mention where that action would be done.

Exercise 2.16

Inglourious Basterds – DVD version

Context: In a French village called Nadine, Lt Raine, his Basterds and Lt Hicox are gathered waiting for action within Operation Kino.

ST: You didn't say the goddamn rendezvous was in a fucking basement.

TT:
No dijo que era en un puto sótano.
[You did not say it was in a fucking basement.]

Taking advantage of the visual channel, the viewer can see that all characters are gathered in a basement. Thus, the subtitler has omitted the phrase 'goddamn rendezvous' [French term for meeting], making use of total reduction, thereby using fewer characters. Albeit 'goddamn' has been omitted, the subtitle does not miss the speaker's tone considering that 'fucking' has been translated literally in the TT.

Exercise 2.17

Velvet Buzzsaw – Netflix

Context: Morf Vandewalt and Josephina are having sex in bed. He opens his eyes and sees a painting that disturbs him, so he has to stop. Josephina then expresses her lack of satisfaction because of this.

ST: We have a fucking problem literally.

TT:
Tenemos un problema de cojones.
[We have a problem of bollocks.]

This subtitle is a good example of a natural rendering of the ST in the TT. Instead of attempting to be faithful to the term 'fucking', the subtitler has used an idiomatic structure which reads *de cojones* [of bollocks], which precedes a noun in Spanish. This is a partial reduction example which shows that literal translation is not usually used and idiomatic structures in the TT are a must in subtitling.

Exercise 2.18

Django Unchained – Netflix
Context: Stephen, a loyal house slave, asks his master and plantation owner Calvin Candie about Django. Stephen is in awe seeing that Django is black and not treated as a slave.
ST: Just who the hell is this "n****r" you feel the need to entertain?
TT: ¿Quién cojones es este negro a quien quieres invitar? [Who the bollocks is this black to whom you want to invite?]

The adverb 'Just' has been eliminated as an unnecessary element. Then the phrase 'who the hell' has been toned up with *Quién cojones* [Who the bollocks]. However, 'n****r' has been translated as *negro* [black]. The fact of talking about someone by referring to his/her skin colour can be considered racist, so we could state that not using further characters to make *negro* sound more offensive has been a solution in terms of economy of characters. Although the racist tone gets toned down.

Exercise 2.19

Sweet Girl – Netflix
Context: Ray Cooper, Rachel's father, is seeking revenge against the pharmaceutical firm which pulled a drug from the market which could have saved his wife from cancer. Ray is threatening Vinod Shah with a gun pointed at his head.
ST: -I know there's others. -You don't have what it takes.
TT: - Hay otros. ¿Quiénes son? - ¿A que no hay huevos? [- There are others. Who are they? - I bet there are no bollocks?]

In this two-liner, a dialogue is uttered by two characters as shown by the hyphens. They are separated with one space from the first letter, but this could be a client's instruction as many other times they are placed next to the following letter. The second exchange has been reformulated by making use of a direct question which uses the phrase *¿A que no hay huevos?* [I bet there are no bollocks?], toning up the TT. We could state that albeit this change from a statement into a direct question is exceptional, it is true that it has given place to a bottom line which has made use of fewer characters than what a closer translation to the ST would have done.

Exercise 2.20

Knives Out – Netflix

Context: Harlan Thrombey, renowned crime novelist, is found dead. Ransom Drysdale, one of the Drysdale siblings, addresses his sister-in-law, Joni Thrombey, disrespectfully over a family argument.

ST: Up your ass, Joni, you've got your teeth bit into this family tit so hard.

TT:
Que te den, Joni.
Llevas mucho tiempo chupando del bote.
[Get given (Fuck you).
You've been a long time living off the boat (this family).]

In this two-liner, we can see a dialogue. In the upper line, 'up your ass' has been translated as *Que te den* [Get given (Fuck you).] which is a milder option of the ST phrase. The second sentence included in the bottom line has been condensed with the chosen sentence as it looks more general and avoids including 'this family tit'. The condensation has been enough to transmit the gist of the conversation.

Chapter 3

Part 1

Exercise 3.1

Fill in the missing words/phrases related to offensive expletives.

Dysphemism	Orthophemism	Euphemism
Fuck!	Ouch!	Fudge!
¡Joder!	¡Ay!	¡Caramba!
Shit!	Oops!	Sugar!
¡Mierda!	¡Oh!	¡Ostras!
Fucking hell!	Oh no!	Yikes!
¡Coño!	¡Oh, no!	¡Ay va!
What the fuck/hell!	What on earth!	What the heck!
¡Qué cojones!	¡Qué me dices!	¡Me cachis (en la mar)!

Exercise 3.2

Fill in the missing words/phrases related to physiological functions.

Dysphemism	Orthophemism	Euphemism
Crapper (Br. Eng.)/ Shitter (Am. Eng.)	Toilet (Br. Eng.)/ Bathroom (Am. Eng.)	Loo
Cagadero	Baño	Tigre
Piss, have a piss (Br. Eng.)/ Take a piss (Am. Eng.)	Urinate	Go to the bathroom
Mear	Miccionar/Orinar	Hacer pis, pipí
Have a shit (Br. Eng.)/ Take a shit (Am. Eng.)/ Shit	Defecate	Go to the bathroom/ Have a bowel movement/ Drop the kids off the pool
Cagar	Defecar	Ir al baño/ Hacer de vientre, cuerpo/ Plantar un pino
Fart	Break wind/Pass gas	Step on a frog/ Cut the cheese/ Rip one
Tirarse un pedo	Ventosear	Tirarse un cuesco

Exercise 3.3

Fill in the missing words/phrases related to sex.

Dysphemism	Orthophemism	Euphemism
Fuck	Have sex	Do it
Follar	Tener sexo	Hacerlo
Screw	Fornicate	Shag (Br. Eng.)/ Knock boots
Joder	Fornicar	
Eat pussy	Cunnilingus	Go down on someone/ Dine at the Y
Comer el coño	Cunnilingus/Sexo oral (fem.)	Bajarse al pilón
Suck dick	Fellatio	Play the skin flute
Comer la polla	Felación/Sexo oral (masc.)	Bajarse al pilón

Exercise 3.4

Fill in the missing words/phrases related to death and mental illness.

Dysphemism	Orthophemism	Euphemism
Die	Pass away/ Pass over/ Pass on	Be gone/ Kick the bucket/ Rest in peace
Morir	Fallecer	Pasar a mejor vida/ Palmarla/ Descansar en paz
Be crazy/Be psychotic	Live with a mental illness	Suffer from nerves
Estar loco	Tener una alteración mental	Estar mal de los nervios
Cripple	Handicapped/Disabled	Challenged/Special
Tullido/a/Lisiado/a	Cojo/a	Paticojo/a
Throw up	Vomit	Puke
Devolver	Vomitar	Echar la pota

Exercise 3.5

Fill in the missing words/phrases related to religion.

Dysphemism	Orthophemism	Euphemism
Oh my God!/ Goddamn it!	My Lord!	Oh my Gosh!/ Oh my goodness!
¡Dios!/ ¡Por los clavos de Cristo!/ ¡Joder!	¡Señor mío!	¡Maldita sea!/ ¡Maldición!
Holy shit!	Good heavens!	For goodness sake!
¡Hostia puta!	¡Por todos los santos!	¡La leche!
Jesus (fucking) Christ!	Good Lord!	Oh my Lord!/ Oh my word!
¡Me cago en la hostia/ Dios!	¡Por el amor de Dios!/ ¡Vaya por Dios!	¡Cachis!/ ¡Me cachis en la mar!/ ¡Pero, bueno!

Exercise 3.6

Fill in the missing words/phrases related to race, sexual conditions and insults.

Dysphemism	Orthophemism	Euphemism
'N****r'/Negro/a	African-American	Person of colour
Negrata/Negro/a de mierda	Afroamericano/a	Persona de color
Dyke	Lesbian/Sapphic	Gay
Tortillera	Lesbiana/Sáfica	Bollera
Queer/Faggot	Homosexual	Gay
Maricón	Homosexual	Mariquita/Mariflor
Whore/Hooker	Prostitute/Sex worker	Promiscuous woman
Puta	Prostituta	Mujer de la vida
Chicken (Am. Eng.)	Prostitute/Sex worker	Gigolo
Puto/Chapero	Prostituto	Gigoló

Part 2

Subtitle the following dialogue exchanges into Spanish carrying out proper segmentation. Also, pay attention to the words in bold type from the ST and specify what category we are dealing with: offensive or taboo and its subcategory.

Note: In real practice, the whole ST should be available to the subtitler because this professional practice entails taking into account both the complete ST and the information provided by the audio and visual channel. However, the exercises presented here are aimed at practising possible renderings of some challenging expressions which have offensive and/or taboo words.

Exercise 3.7

The Hateful Eight – DVD version	
Context: Major Marquis tells General Sandy Smithers how he made his son suffer before killing him naked in the snow.	
ST: and I stuck **my big, black Johnson** right down his goddamn throat.	
TT:	Saqué **mi enorme polla negra** del pantalón [I took **my enormous black cock** out of the trousers]
Category/subcategory: Taboo/sex	

This subtitle is composed of two lines. The sexual-related taboo term used is 'my big, black Johnson', which in slang concerns his penis and has been translated in more open terms as can be seen in *mi enorme polla negra* [my enormous black cock]. The character speaking refers to the fact that his penis is black and big to alarm the addressee, who is an old white man and whose son suffered at the character's hands.

Exercise 3.8

Reservoir Dogs – DVD version
Context: Mr Blonde enters the warehouse and more arguments and quarrelling ensue.
ST: You're acting like **a bunch of fucking "n****rs"**, man!

TT:
            Os comportáis
            como **un par de negros**.
            [You behave
            like **a couple of black guys**.]

Category/subcategory: Offensive/insult

This example shows how 'fucking "n****rs"' is transferred by using a phrase which is much milder than the original, *negros* [black guys]. In fact, the phrase gets amplified with the use of 'fucking' and also because the word is said by a white character and not among Afro-American characters. This is a case in which the cultural load of 'n****rs' needs to be considered carefully so that the impact of the term does not get lost in the TT. We could assume there was no room for more characters or the subtitler opted for using *negro* [black] to preserve lexical consistency. In terms of categories, we could state that it is a race-related insult. As for the segmentation, the line break of the two-liner is correct as the bottom line has the complement of the verb.

Exercise 3.9

Nine Perfect Strangers SE01 EP05 – Prime Video
Context: While having breakfast at the table, Lars Lee tells everyone about a strange dream he had. Lars says Tony Hogburn was in it and receives the following reply.
ST: -You're **a fucking lunatic**. -You know that, Lars?

TT:
    - Estás **como una cabra**, ¿lo sabes Lars?
    - Sí, lo sé.
    [- You are **like a goat**, do you know it, Lars?
    - Yes, I know it.]

Category/subcategory: Offensive/insult

'Fucking lunatic' has been transferred as *como una cabra* [like a goat], which in the TT is used to express that someone is crazy. However, this is a euphemistic formula which is milder than the original phrase, which also has 'fucking', not used in the TT either, although the gist of the phrase is visible in the TT. This could be categorised as an offensive term in the form of an insult. As a two-liner, the segmentation shows there are two exchanges from different speakers which are put in their corresponding lines.

Exercise 3.10

Pulp Fiction – DVD version
Context: A young man with an English accent and his girlfriend are sitting in an LA coffee shop where they will try to rob all the customers and employees.
ST: Normally **both your asses** would be **dead as fucking fried chicken**.
TT: Normalmente,   ambos estaríais **como un pollo frito**,   [Normally,   both would be **like a fried chicken**,]
Category/subcategory: Offensive/violence

There are two different terms/phrases to consider here. First, 'asses' is a slang term, which in English is used to refer to a person in a vulgar way. It has been omitted in the subtitle. Next, 'dead as fucking fried chicken' is used as a violent term that is employed when someone is killed. In this case, it is even stronger with the addition of 'fucking'. Its transfer is milder as we can see in the euphemistic phrase *pollo frito* [fried chicken]. The segmentation is correct, as the adverb of frequency followed by the comma is placed in the top line and the rest of the sentence is in the bottom line.

Exercise 3.11

Succession SE03 EP09 – HBO
Context: The Roy siblings are in Italy for their mother's wedding. Also present is their father and CEO of the firm, Logan Roy. Tom Wambsgans, Shiv's husband, is talking to Greg Hirsch disrespectfully.
ST: "Uh, but I don't recall, Your Honor, I don't recall...". **You're a fucking joke**, man.
TT: "No lo recuerdo, señoría...".   **Eres patético, joder.**   ["I don't remember it, your honour...".   **You're pathetic, fuck.**]
Category/subcategory: Offensive/insult

The insult 'You're a fucking joke' is visible in the subtitle with other words, which keeps the tone out of it. The phrase *Eres patético* [You're pathetic] is emphasised with the addition of the word *joder* [fuck], placed at the end of the utterance. As we can see, the subtitler has had to change the syntax of the sentence in favour of providing the audience with a natural expression. Regarding the segmentation, in the top line we can see a quote which finishes and then a different exchange in the bottom line.

Exercise 3.12

Inglourious Basterds – DVD version
Context: In a French village called Nadine, Lt Raine, his Basterds and Lt Hicox are gathered waiting for action within Operation Kino.
ST: This **Jerry** of yours, Stiglitz, not exactly the **loquacious** type, is he?
TT: Ese **fritz** suyo, Stiglitz...   No es que sea muy **locuaz**, ¿no?   [That **fritz** of yours, Stiglitz...   He is not very **loquacious**, is he?]
Category/subcategory: Offensive/insult   Category/subcategory: Offensive/invective

We have two cases for discussion here. First, the term 'Jerry' was an offensive slang term given to the Germans during World War II by the Allied soldiers and civilians, especially the British. Although originally created during World War I, it was not commonly used until World War II. The term is meant to play on the shape of the German helmet, which resembled a jerry, a British slang word for a chamber pot. It is translated as 'fritz', a German nickname for Friedrich – another name given to the German troops by the British and others during the world wars (Allen, 1983). This is a case of an offensive slur, and the subtitler has preferred to resort to the loan 'fritz', which has more chances of being recognised by the target culture because of its Germanic root; in other words, an insult. Second, the invective 'the loquacious type' has been literally subtitled as *locuaz* [loquacious], thereby preserving the hidden and more direct insult the viewer can think of. As for the segmentation, two different sentences are placed in their corresponding lines.

Exercise 3.13

Pulp Fiction – DVD version
Context: In a club, Butch Coolidge, a prizefighter, meets Marsellus Wallace as they are going to prepare a boxing fight where he must be beaten by a knockout.
ST: When you kicking it in the Caribbean,
TT: cuando estés en el Caribe   viviendo **como Dios**,   [when you are in the Caribbean   living **like God**,]
Category/subcategory: No offensive *or* Taboo category

This is a particular case as the ST does not include any offensive or taboo element. However, the TT reads *vivendo como Dios* [living like God] and to a religious person's ears, this can be mildly strong as God is not to be mentioned in vain. Thus, we can observe how subtitlers sometimes compensate for some omissions of offensive/taboo elements by using them later in some way. Regarding the segmentation, the second clause has been placed in the bottom line correctly.

Answer Key 115

Exercise 3.14

Narcos: Mexico SE03 EP05 – Netflix

Context: DEA agent Walt Breslin is talking to other agents about the Mexican Cartels and then he reacts after some information is given to the group.

ST: Are you **fucking** kidding me?

TT:

¡**Hostia puta**!
[**Fucking host (hell)**!]

Category/subcategory: Offensive/swear word

We can observe that there is an offensive term in the form of 'fucking'. Aiming to use an idiomatic phrase in the TT, the subtitler has resorted to blasphemy which intensifies the tone given with *¡Hostia puta!* [Fucking host (hell)!], with some religious connotations that a catholic audience would notice.

Exercise 3.15

Once Upon a Time in Hollywood – DVD version

Context: Rick Dalton and his stunt double Cliff Booth are driving. They stop at a traffic light and Rick insults a group of hippies he sees on the street.

ST: **Fucking** hippie **motherfuckers**.

TT:

Malditos hippies, **hijos de puta**.
[**Bloody** hippies, **sons of bitch**.]

Category/subcategory: Offensive/insult

This is a clear example of how the ST can be very closely transferred to the TT, producing an idiomatic phrase. The derogatory adjective 'fucking' emphasises the insult to hippies with the second intensifying element 'motherfuckers'. The result in the subtitle, *Malditos hippies, hijos de puta* [Bloody hippies, sons of bitch], keeps that load and sounds idiomatic for the target audience.

Exercise 3.16

Once Upon a Time in Hollywood – DVD version

Context: Rick Dalton has a conversation with filmmaker Sam Wanamaker.

ST: -**Goddamn it. I fucked this** whole thing up, Sam. -Keep going.

TT:

-**Mierda, lo estoy jodiendo**, Sam.
-Sigue adelante, Rick.
[-**Shit, I'm fucking it (screwing it up)**, Sam.
-Go ahead, Rick.]

Category/subcategory: Offensive/curse
Category/subcategory: Offensive/swear word

Here, we have two cases under analysis. First, the cursing 'Goddamn it' in the ST is visible in the TT in the form of the term *Mierda* [Shit]. Second, the swear phrase 'I fucked it' is also transferred to the subtitle by means of the same subcategory. All in all, the intensity of the original can be said to be present in the TT. With regard to the segmentation, each of the different characters' exchanges are placed in the different lines of this two-liner.

Exercise 3.17

The White Lotus SE01 EP01 – HBO
Context: On a boat trip in Hawaii, Olivia Mossbacher and her friend Paula fantasise about the lives of the recently married couple Shane and Rachel Patton.
ST: -She loves him, but… -**He's got a small dick.**
TT: 　　　　　-Ella lo quiere, pero… 　　　　　-**La tiene pequeña.** 　　　　[-She loves him, but… 　　　　-He's got it small.]
Category/subcategory: Taboo/sex *or* Offensive/insult

The sexual-related taboo term in the dialogue appears as 'dick'. It is visible in the subtitle by means of condensation because instead of including the term again, it uses a pronoun to use fewer characters, *La tiene* [He's got it]. In the TL, it is a recurrent formula to refer to a male's penis. In addition, the fact of talking about someone having a small penis has negative connotations to some males' perception, for which reason, we could state that the phrase can be categorised as an insult as well. This segmentation contains every exchange in the different lines of this two-liner.

Exercise 3.18

Succession SE03 EP09 – HBO
Context: Logan Roy is talking to Lukas Matsson about the possibility of selling his company to him. Logan emigrated from Scotland to America and describes what America looks like now.
ST: Now look at them, **fat as fuck, scrawny on meth** or yoga.
TT: 　　　　Míralos ahora. O **gordos como vacas** 　　　　o **esmirriados por la meta** o el yoga. 　　　[Look at them now. Either **fat as cows** 　　　　or **bony on meth** or yoga.]
Category/subcategory: Offensive/insult Category/subcategory: Taboo/drugs consumption

The first phrase under analysis is 'fat as fuck', which is subtitled as *gordos como vacas* [fat as cows]. It can be considered an insult as it concerns one's physical condition. The second phrase, 'scrawny on meth', subtitled as *esmirriados por la meta* [bony on meth], relates to drug consumption for which reason it can be considered taboo. As for the segmentation, we can see a clause in the top line and then the second one starts with the conjunction *o* [or], as is usually carried out with copulative sentences.

Exercise 3.19

Succession SE03 EP09 – HBO
Context: Kendall Roy is having a meltdown in front of his siblings Shiv and Roman. He confesses something very serious that happened.
ST: **I killed** a kid.
TT: **Maté** a un chaval. [**I killed** a kid.]
Category/subcategory: Offensive/violence

In this case, the verb 'killed' is killing or violence related, which informs about a murder. This subcategory is considered offensive given the implications that are derived from someone revealing having committed a crime, which concerns taking someone's life away.

Exercise 3.20

Pulp Fiction – DVD version
Context: Vincent goes out with Marsellus' wife, Mia, for dinner.
ST: **What the fuck** is this place?
TT: ¿**Qué coño** es este sitio? [**What the cunt (fuck)** is this place?]
Category/subcategory: Offensive/swear word

The recurrent interrogative pronoun 'What the fuck' has been subtitled as *¿Qué coño?* [What the cunt (fuck)?]. The chosen phrase is very common in the TL and even though other formulas can be employed, it can be said to be quite balanced. The use of a wh-word plus the phrase 'the fuck' is very much used in cases of surprise or to release anger.

Exercise 3.21

The White Lotus SE01 EP06 – HBO
Context: Staying at a fancy resort in Hawaii, recently married Shane Patton complains to reception because someone has defecated in his suitcase in the room where he and his wife are staying.
ST: Yeah, I'm in the Pineapple Suite, and there's **a fucking turd** in my room.
TT: y hay **un zurullo** en mi habitación, **joder**. [and there's **a turd** in my room, **fuck**.]
Category/subcategory: Taboo/scatology

The scatology-related taboo term in this case is reinforced by the term 'fucking'. It has been transferred to the subtitle as *un zurullo* [a turd], which in both languages is a euphemism for 'shit'. In order to also make use of the term 'fucking', the subtitler has placed it at the end of the utterance through the word *joder* [fuck] as an expletive. The segmentation places the main sentence in the top line, followed by the expletive which closes the utterance without breaking any syntactic or semantic unit.

Exercise 3.22

Once Upon a Time in Hollywood – DVD version
Context: Filmmaker Randy Miller talks to Rick Dalton about his stunt double and a wardrobe assistant.
ST: […] and, man, she's a **fucking bitch**. I just don't. Please, I…
TT: y es una **cabrona de la hostia**. No me… Por favor. [and she is a **fucker of the host (fucking bastard)**. Don't me… Please.]
Category/subcategory: Offensive/insult

There is an insult strengthened by the addition of the f-word in the phrase 'fucking bitch'. It is transferred to the subtitle in the form of a different rendering: *cabrona de la hostia* [fucker of the host (fucking bastard)]. The phrase chosen in the TT is idiomatic, which is perfectly understood by the target audience and has the same offensive subcategory. The segmentation starts after a full stop, so the exchanges are properly separated.

Exercise 3.23

Sweet Girl – Netflix
Context: Detective John Rothman is surprised after reading a note and Detective Sarah Meeker wants to know about it.
ST: -**Holy shit**! -What?
TT: - ¡**Hostia**! - ¿Qué? [- **Host (Fuck)**! - What?]
Category/subcategory: Offensive/expletive

Here, we observe the expletive 'Holy shit!'. The translation has been carried out through an equivalent in the form of a religious-related taboo word, *¡Hostia!* [Host (Fuck)!], which is strong in Spanish as it refers to the body of Christ or the Eucharistic bread for Catholics. However, it could also be argued that it is an expletive used in moments of surprise, for which reason the religious semantic load can be lost, but it would keep its offensive load. The two exchanges are shown in two different lines of this two-liner.

Exercise 3.24

Knives Out – Netflix

Context: Harlan Thrombey, renowned crime novelist, is found dead and his family are being interrogated by Detective Benoit Blanc, who asks Richard Drysdale about his father.

ST: -Did he get into the party? [...] -**Oh my God!**

TT:
> ¡Vaya que sí!
> [Yes, of course!]

Category/subcategory: Taboo/profanity

    Here, we see the profanity 'Oh my God!'. When subtitled into Spanish, it loses its strong connotation given that the chosen equivalent has no taboo or offensive connotations, *¡Vaya que sí!* [Yes, of course!]. However, we could argue that the TT fits in with the conversation that is taking place in the scene. This idea supports the fact that subtitlers do not transfer isolated exchanges, but the gist of the whole dialogue.

Exercise 3.25

Deadpool 2 – DVD version

Context: Colossus throws Deadpool from a wheelchair because the latter does not stop talking and ignores Colossus' advice.

ST: **What the fuck!**

TT:
> ¡Me cago en la puta!
> [I shit on the whore (Fucking hell)!]

Category/subcategory: Offensive/expletive *or* swear phrase

    The expletive *What the fuck!* is subtitled by means of a recurrent phrase in the TL, which is *¡Me cago en la puta!* [I shit on the whore (Fucking hell)!]. It functions as an equivalent of the offensive tone of the ST and it is of note that it is a recurrent Spanish expression when subtitling religious profane or blasphemous exchanges. As some subcategories sometimes overlap, we could also categorise it as a swear phrase.

Exercise 3.26

Succession SE03 EP08 – HBO

Context: Gerri Kellman has some words with Roman Roy to let him know that his behaviour is far from acceptable.

ST: -I need you to stop sending me the items. [...] -You don't want pictures of **my dick**. -No.

TT:
> - ¿No quieres fotos de **mi polla**?
> - No.
> [Don't you want pictures of **my dick**?
> - No.]

Category/subcategory: Taboo/sex

Talking about sex or sexual body parts is a common topic in taboo language. In this example, the sexual reference we can see in 'my dick' has been transferred to the subtitle in similar terms: *mi polla* [my dick]. In these cases, faithful translations tend to work well for the target audience. The two-liner is the subtitle used to give room to two characters' exchanges.

Exercise 3.27

Deadpool 2 – DVD version
Context: Deadpool asks Colossus a question.
ST: Why can't I **fucking die**?
TT:
¿Por qué **coño** no puedo **morir**? [Why the cunt (fuck) can't I die?]
Category/subcategory: Offensive/swear word

In this example, the offensive term 'fucking' is emphasising the taboo verb 'die'. We could argue that the exchange is offensive because of the use of 'fucking'. However, talking about dying can also be a taboo topic depending on the context and the reason. All in all, the transfer has been made in similar terms with the use of *¿Por qué coño...?* [Why the cunt (fuck)...?] and *morir* [die].

Exercise 3.28

Snatch – DVD version
Context: Cousin Avi Denovitz is having an argument with Doug the Head about the way they are going to do business.
ST: -Avi! -Shut up and sit down, you **bald fuck**!
TT:
- ¡Avi!   - ¡Calla y siéntate, **calvo mamón**!   [- Avi!   - Shut up and sit down, **bald prick**!]
Category/subcategory: Offensive/insult

This dialogue includes the insult 'bald fuck'. Albeit the word 'fuck' is a strong insult in English and is reinforced by the physical aspect depicted by 'bald', its rendering in the TT is somehow milder as it reads *calvo mamón* [bald prick]. As for the segmentation, as there is a dialogue between two speakers, we can see a two-liner.

Exercise 3.29

The Hateful Eight – DVD version

Context: In a shelter in cold Wyoming winter, O. B. Jackon and Sheriff Chris Mannix try to hammer two pieces of wood on the door to keep it from opening because of the wind. Joe Gage and Daisy Domergue yell at them to be heard because the wind is very loud.

ST: -**Goddamn it to hell**! -Gonna open if you don't…

TT:
-¡**Me cago en todo**!
-¡Se abrirá si no la cla…!
[-**I shit on everything (Fuck it all)**!
-It'll get open if you don't…!]

Category/subcategory: Offensive/curse *or* expletive

The phrase 'Goddamn it to hell!' is a curse and therefore an offensive expression similar to an expletive, which could be another interpretation for the subcategory of this offensive expression. It has been transferred to the subtitle by means of a taboo expression related to scatology, *¡Me cago en todo!* [I shit on everything (Fuck it all)!]. This Spanish expression is very common when the speaker wants to express surprise or anger. Again, we see a two-liner as there are two exchanges from different speakers.

Exercise 3.30

Once Upon a Time in Hollywood – DVD version

Context: Stunt double Cliff Booth has a fight with a young hippy man and threatens a group of his female friends who want to approach Cliff about defending their friend.

ST: Come one step closer and **I will knock his teeth out**.

TT:
Un paso más
y **le salto las muelas**.
[One more step
and **I will knock his molars out**.]

Category/subcategory: Offensive/violence

Here, we see a violence-related offensive expression in 'I will knock his teeth out'. It has been transferred to the TT in very similar terms, with the exception of the change of 'teeth' to *muelas* [molars], which does not prevent the audience from observing this violent threat.

Chapter 4

Subtitle the following dialogue exchanges into Spanish carrying out proper segmentation. Then, think about the category and subcategory of offensive and taboo in the ST, written in bold type. Next, think of the possible translation strategy used during the translation operations and specify the technique, that is, if the translation load has been transferred (toned up, maintained or toned down) or not transferred (neutralised or omitted).

Note: In real practice, the whole ST should be available to the subtitler because this professional practice entails taking into account both the complete ST and the information provided by the audio and visual channel. However, the exercises presented here are aimed at practising possible renderings of some challenging expressions which have offensive and/or taboo words.

Exercise 4.1

Narcos: Mexico SE03 EP05 – Netflix

Context: DEA agent Walt Breslin talks to his superior James Kuykendall.

ST: With all due respect, Sir, I'm here **to get shit done.**

TT:
    Con todo el respecto, señor,
    he venido a trabajar.
    [With all due respect, Sir,
    I have come to work.]

Category/subcategory: Taboo/scatology
Strategy/technique: Omission/Non-transfer (load omitted)

Here, the scatological-related taboo term 'shit', visible in the ST, has been omitted in the subtitle. Thus, the technique used is non-transfer as the load of the term has been deleted. Note that the term 'shit' is very common in vulgar oral English. The subtitler was probably forced to condense the ST due to spatiotemporal constraints.

Exercise 4.2

Succession SE03 EP08 – HBO

Context: Stewy Hosseini and Sandi Furness meet Logan Roy, Roman Roy and Tom Wambsgans at an office in their company building to discuss some business.

ST: Great. We're all over the **fucking** moon. What is this?

TT:
    Genial, estamos todos encantados.
    No me jodas.
    [Great, we are all delighted.
    Don't fuck me.]

Category/subcategory: Offensive/swear word
Strategy/technique: Compensation/Transfer (load maintained)

The swear word 'fucking' has not been included in the same sentence as the original. This is an example of compensation because the term has been transferred in the next phrase, being reformulated differently, but transferring the load of the original in the TT phrase *No me jodas* [Don't fuck me.].

Exercise 4.3

Deadpool 2 – DVD version
Context: Deadpool talks to a group of Japanese gangs with whom he is fighting.
ST: I don't bargain, **pumpkin fucker**.

TT:
    'Yo no negocio, **follacabras**'.
    ['I don't negotiate, **goat-shagger**'.]

Category/subcategory: Offensive/insult Strategy/technique: Lexical recreation/Transfer (load maintained)

As some insults do not have a direct equivalent between some languages, lexical recreation works very well in these cases. As we can read in the original, the insult 'pumpkin fucker' has been transferred via the lexical recreation *follacabras* [goat-shagger], although in English the phrase commonly used is 'sheep-shagger'. The TT term in Spanish is not recognised by the RAE [Royal Spanish Academy], but is easily understood by the target culture, while the transfer maintains the load of the term in the ST.

Exercise 4.4

Succession SE03 EP08 – HBO
Context: Stewy Hosseini and Sandi Furness meet Logan Roy, Roman Roy and Tom Wambsgans at an office in their company building to discuss some business.
ST: -Matsson's a visionary. -Sure. Because **he's tripping balls**.

TT:
    -Matsson es un visionario.
    -Ya. Porque **siempre va puesto**.
    [-Matsson is a visionary.
    -Yes. Because **he is always high**.]

Category/subcategory: Taboo/drugs consumption Strategy/technique: Substitution/Transfer (load toned down)

The expression 'tripping balls' is a slang phrase referring to someone intoxicated by a psychoactive drug. The phrase chosen by the subtitler to describe this taboo verb is *siempre va puesto* [he's always high], which in Spanish is a toned-down expression when talking about someone consuming drugs. We can therefore state that the transfer is visible in the TT.

Exercise 4.5

Succession SE03 EP08 – HBO

Context: Logan Roy meets his son Kendall over dinner and they have a serious conversation about Kendall's addictions.

ST: ...and whenever you **fucked up**, I cleaned up **your shit**.

TT:
> Y, cuando **tú la cagabas**,
> [And, when **you shitted it (screwed it up)**,]
>
> yo solucionaba tus marrones.
> [I fixed your browns (problems).]

Category/subcategory: Offensive/swear word
Strategy/technique: Literal translation/Transfer (load maintained)

Category/subcategory: Taboo/scatology
Strategy/technique: Substitution/Non-transfer (load neutralised)

In the first subtitle, the verb 'fucked up' has been very closely translated with the phrase *tú la cagabas* [shitted it (screwed it up)]. Thus, the offensive load has been transferred. As for the second subtitle, the phrase 'your shit' has been substituted with *tus marrones* [your browns (problems)], which neutralises the load of 'your shit'. Therefore, this is an example of non-transfer because of the loss of the effect of the ST phrase, which vanishes in the TT.

Exercise 4.6

Deadpool 2 – DVD version

Context: Deadpool has a conversation with his wife Vanessa and asks her a question.

ST: I don't know what this is.

TT:
> ¿**Qué coño** es esto?
> [**What the cunt (fuck)** is this?]

Category/subcategory: No offensive *or* Taboo category
Strategy/technique: Compensation/Transfer (load toned up)

There are cases when the ST has no offensive or taboo elements, as is the case in this example. The subtitler resorts to compensation probably because, previously, some offensive or taboo load could not be included. Thus, we find the question *¿Qué coño...?* [What the cunt (fuck)...?], which peppers the subtitle with a swear word, toning up the ST statement.

Exercise 4.7

Snatch – DVD version

Context: Mickey O'Neil is fighting Gorgeous George in a stable. Mickey tells Gorgeous George the following before knocking him down.

ST: **Deadly kick** for a **fat fucker**, you know that?

TT:
Te hostiaré, gordo mamón.
[I'll fucking beat you up, fat prick.]

Category/subcategory: Offensive/violence
Strategy/technique: Reformulation/Transfer (load toned up)

Category/subcategory: Offensive/insult
Strategy/technique: Substitution/Transfer (load maintained)

This example presents two challenges. First, the violent phrase 'Deadly kick' has been reformulated in such a way that the load has been toned up in the subtitle, as seen in *Te hostiaré* [I'll fucking beat you up]. Second, the insult 'fat fucker' could be said to have been transferred while maintaining its load in general terms. Albeit 'fucker' has been substituted with *mamón* [prick], which is milder in Spanish, we can argue that the insult has a double load with the term *gordo* [fat], for which reason we can support that the transfer of the ST has been made possible in the subtitle.

Exercise 4.8

Succession SE03 EP08 – HBO

Context: The Roy siblings are in Italy for their mother's wedding. Also present is their father and CEO of the firm, Logan Roy. Roman is talking to Shiv, Tom and Gerri about business.

ST: Yeah, my goodness, gummy love bite from the **fucking** toddlers.

TT:
Sí, Dios mío.
Una gominola de parte de los bebés.
[Yes, my God.
A gummy from the toddlers.]

Category/subcategory: Offensive/swear word
Strategy/technique: Omission/Non-transfer (load omitted)

Let us focus on the euphemism 'my goodness' of the ST. The goal of that phrase is not to mention God, but the TT includes *Dios mío* [my God], which in the target culture is not considered offensive in these terms. As for 'fucking', as it has been omitted in the subtitle, this is a case of non-transfer. However, we can observe that the ST is rather long, for which reason the subtitler might have had to condense it, omitting 'fucking' in favour of abiding by the space and time restrictions.

Exercise 4.9

Knives Out – Netflix

Context: Harlan Thrombey, renowned crime novelist, is found dead and his family are being interrogated by Detective Benoit Blanc. Marta Cabrera is talking to Benoit and Meg Thrombey mutters.

ST: No, it's not okay. **What the hell!**

TT:

No, sí que pasa. **¡No me jodas!**
[No, it does happen. **Don't fuck me!**]

Category/subcategory: Offensive/expletive
Strategy/technique: Reformulation/Transfer (load toned up)

The mild expletive 'What the hell!' has been reformulated by making use of a stronger exclamation, which is *¡No me jodas!* [Don't fuck me!]. This transfer of the ST provides the subtitle with a load that has been toned up, giving more character to the speaker's speech.

Exercise 4.10

Knives Out – Netflix

Context: Harlan Thrombey, renowned crime novelist, is found dead and his family are being interrogated by Detective Benoit Blanc. Linda Drysdale addresses Marta Cabrera insulting her.

ST: Oh you **little bitch**!

TT:

¡La muy cabrona!
[**The very fucker (What a fucker)!**]

Category/subcategory: Offensive/insult
Strategy/technique: Reformulation/Transfer (load maintained)

The insult present in the ST, 'little bitch', has been reformulated in the TT in the form of *¡La muy cabrona!* [The very fucker (What a fucker)!]. This is a clear example of the multiple renderings that reformulation allows subtitlers to transfer the load of a term or phrase causing a similar effect in the target audience. Idiomatic phrases over literal renderings normally prevail when dealing with the transfer of offensive and taboo terms.

Exercise 4.11

Knives Out – Netflix

Context: Harlan Thrombey, renowned crime novelist, is found dead and his family are being interrogated by Detective Benoit Blanc. Walt Thrombey answers Benoit's question about the night of the party.

ST: No, **Jesus**. We did not get into it.

TT:

¡Qué va! No nos encaramos.
[No way! We didn't confront each other.]

Category/subcategory: Taboo/profanity
Strategy/technique: Reformulation/Non-transfer (load neutralised)

As already discussed, mentioning God or Jesus in vain has strong connotations for Catholics in the English-speaking culture. The ST includes the profanity 'Jesus', whose taboo load is not transferred to the TT as it is neutralised with the rendering *¡Qué va!* [No way!]. This does not mean that the subtitler's choice is inappropriate; it just means that the load this religious referent has in this source culture and language has been left out.

Exercise 4.12

Knives Out – Netflix

Context: Harlan Thrombey, renowned crime novelist, is found dead and his family are being interrogated by Detective Benoit Blanc. Ransom Drysdale addresses Detective Benoit Blanc disrespectfully after feeling threatened by the detective's words.

ST: Shut up with **that Kentucky-fried, Foghorn Leghorn drawl!**

TT:
¡Que es usted un **ridículo** y un **pedante**!
[That you are **ridiculous** and **pedantic**!]

Category/subcategory: Offensive/invective
Strategy/technique: Transposition/Transfer (load maintained)

This example shows an invective or subtle insult in the TT, visible in 'that Kentucky-fried, Foghorn Leghorn drawl!'. This is a reference to Looney Tunes' Southern rooster Foghorn Leghorn when referring to the speaker's particular accent. The subtitler opted for transposition which transmits the way the character talks by using the adjectives *ridículo* [ridiculous] and *pedante* [pedant]. Thus, the transfer of the invective materialises in the subtitle as words understandable by the target audience.

Exercise 4.13

Narcos: Mexico SE03 EP01 – Netflix

Context: DEA agent Walt Breslin tries to calm Mike down after revealing to him that he is an undercover agent.

ST: I need you to **shut the fuck up** and calm down.

TT:
Necesito que cierres el pico y te calmes.
[I need you to close the pick (shut up) and calm down.]

Category/subcategory: Offensive/swear phrase
Strategy/technique: Omission/Non-transfer (load omitted)

The phrase 'the fuck' commonly accompanies the verb 'to shut up' when a speaker swears. In this case, the phrase has not been transferred to the TT as it has been omitted. However, in terms of naturalness or idiomaticity, the subtitler has used the expression *cierres el pico* [close the pick (shut up)], which draws a comparison between a person's mouth and a bird's pick, providing the rendering with a slang tone, which seems to be very appropriate for the conversation taking place in the scene.

Exercise 4.14

Deadpool 2 – DVD version

Context: Colossus has grabbed Deadpool by the neck because he does not pay enough attention to him. Deadpool complains after being released.

ST: Oh, **Jesus Christ**!

TT:

¡**Su puta madre**!
[**His fucking mother**!]

Category/subcategory: Taboo/blasphemy
Strategy/technique: Substitution/Transfer (load maintained)

The recurrent blasphemy 'Jesus Christ' has been reformulated maintaining the load this phrase has in the original, but with a change of subcategory as we can see in *¡Su puta madre!* [His fucking mother!]. This is a very common offensive phrase in the target culture which contains offensive terms, but avoids offending a religious audience. The phrase in the TT is commonly used without being aimed at anyone, but as a way to release anger.

Exercise 4.15

Deadpool 2 – DVD version

Context: Deadpool is being given a ride by Dopinder, a taxi driver. The former asks the latter a question.

ST: What's your poison? A little, uh, **cokey, cokey**.

TT:

¿Cuál es tu vicio? ¿Te va **el perico**?
[What's your vice? Do you like **the blow**?]

Category/subcategory: Taboo/drugs consumption
Strategy/technique: Substitution/Transfer (load toned down)

In the ST, we see 'cokey', which is a slang word for someone who is a cocaine addict. Instead of translating this noun more closely, the subtitler has opted for a more specific term via substitution, that is, by using the drug rather than the person who consumes it. The term used in Spanish, *el perico* [the blow], is a milder one to refer to cocaine. Thus, we could argue that the TT has been toned down, but the gist has been transferred to the audience with this translation operation.

Exercise 4.16

Reservoir Dogs – DVD version

Context: The film begins with eight men in black having breakfast at a café, Mr White, Mr Pink, Mr Blue, Mr Blonde, Mr Orange, Mr Brown, the big boss Joe Cabot and his son Nice Guy Eddie Cabot.

ST: Never mind what you normally would do.

TT:

Lo que hagas normalmente
me importa una mierda.
[What you normally do
bothers me shit.]

Category/subcategory: No offensive *or* Taboo category
Strategy/technique: Compensation/Transfer (load toned up)

There are no offensive or taboo elements in the ST. However, there are in the TT. 'Never mind' has been rendered as *me importa una mierda* [bothers me shit]. This is an example in which compensation may have taken place to balance some previous offensive or taboo element missed out or just to make the subtitle stronger with a taboo word, depicting the speaker's way of talking.

Exercise 4.17

Knives Out – Netflix
Context: Harlan Thrombey, renowned crime novelist, is found dead and his family are being interrogated by Detective Benoit Blanc. He talks to all the family defending Marta Cabrera over their accusations towards their father's death.
ST: You have all treated her **like shit** to steal back a fortune that you lost and she deserves.
TT: La han tratado fatal [You've treated her terribly.] para quitarle la fortuna que ustedes han perdido y ella se merece. [to take from her the fortune that you have lost and she deserves.]
Category/subcategory: Taboo/scatology Strategy/technique: Substitution/Non-transfer (load neutralised)

Condensation is paramount when the ST is very wordy. In this example, the phrase 'like shit' has been substituted with a shorter term, *fatal* [terribly]. Although that term has not been transferred because it has been neutralised, the subtitler has been able to condense the ST in the two subtitles included in the example, transmitting the information provided by the screenplay.

Exercise 4.18

Deadpool 2 – DVD version
Context: Deadpool is moaning to Blind Al, who tries to cheer him up.
ST: It's a little hard to hear you with **that pity dick in your mouth**.
TT: No te oigo bien con **esa polla llorona en la boca**. [I can't hear you well with **that crying dick in your mouth**.]
Category/subcategory: Taboo/sex Strategy/technique: Literal translation/Transfer (load maintained)

The sex-related phrase in this ST, 'pity dick in your mouth', has been translated literally as *esa polla llorona en la boca* [that crying dick in your mouth]. The load of the phrase has been transferred to the TT. As can be seen here, some faithful renderings can work well with taboo expressions.

Exercise 4.19

Pulp Fiction – DVD version

Context: Mia, thinking she is going to inhale cocaine, takes an overdose of Vince's heroin powder. Vince tries to save her life with Lance, his drug dealer's help.

ST: Oh, **Jesus fucking Christ**!

TT:
¡**Me cago en la puta**!
[I shit on the whore (Fucking hell)!]

Category/subcategory: Taboo/blasphemy
Strategy/technique: Substitution/Transfer (load maintained)

This example is a challenging case of blasphemy. The blasphemy 'Jesus fucking Christ' has been substituted with another offensive element, whose tone can be said to be balanced although it is not religious related. This is usually the case with professional subtitles as self-censorship can take place given the impact that written language has over oral language.

Exercise 4.20

Succession SE03 EP08 – HBO

Context: Shiv and her brother Roman are having a conversation on a private jet. He proposes some idea regarding her mother's soon-to-be wedding which she rejects.

ST: **Fuck it**.

TT:
Me la suda.
[It sweats me it (I don't give a damn).]

Category/subcategory: Offensive/swear word
Strategy/technique: Reformulation/Transfer (load toned down)

Here, we have an offensive phrase, 'Fuck it', which has been reformulated in a softened way with *Me la suda* [It sweats me it (I don't give a damn)]. This expression is a euphemism of *me suda la polla* [It sweats my dick!], usually uttered by males to express in a vulgar way that they do not care about something. In any case, the load of the ST has been transferred to the TT.

Exercise 4.21

Deadpool 2 – DVD version

Context: Deadpool has a conversation with barman Weasel at the bar.

ST: And nobody **fucking** realizes it.

TT:
Y nadie lo pilla, **cojones**.
[And nobody gets it, **bollocks**.]

Category/subcategory: Offensive/swear word
Strategy/technique: Substitution/Transfer (load maintained)

'Fucking', one of the most recurrent derivatives of the f-word, has been translated in an idiomatic way via substitution. The transfer has therefore been possible through the term *cojones* [bollocks]. Sometimes, it is not possible to faithfully translate 'fucking' because of the differences between English and Spanish and this is one of those cases.

Exercise 4.22

Once Upon a Time in Hollywood – DVD version
Context: Filmmaker Randy Miller tells stunt double Cliff Booth to get dressed for some film shooting.
ST: Okay, you **fucking horse's ass**. Let's get you over to wardrobe.
TT: Vale tú, **soplapollas**. Vamos a vestuario. [Okay, you **cock blower (cocksucker)**. Let's go to the wardrobe.]
Category/subcategory: Offensive/insult Strategy/technique: Substitution/Transfer (load maintained)

The insult 'fucking horse's ass' has been substituted with another offensive element in the form of the insult *soplapollas* [cock blower (cocksucker)], which is used to refer to someone who is stupid or dumb. It can be observed that the original contains a double insult ('fucking' and 'horse's ass'), but as we already know, subtitling entails condensation and the insult in the ST appears in the TT with a different term.

Exercise 4.23

Deadpool 2 – DVD version
Context: The film begins with Deadpool committing suicide by blowing himself to pieces. While flying through the air, he says some words to Wolverine.
ST: Fuck Wolverine. [...] Then **the hairy motherfucker** ups the ante by dying.
TT: Y luego va **el puto barbitas** y se tira el moco y la espicha. [And then **the fucking beardy** goes and shows off and dies.]
Category/subcategory: Offensive/insult Strategy/technique: Substitution/Transfer (load maintained)

The insult 'the hairy motherfucker' has been transferred via substitution in the TT. It can be observed that the use of *puto* [fucking] in the TT has fewer characters than a more literal rendering of 'motherfucker'. Also, the use of *barbitas* [beardy] is in line with Deadpool's humorous tone, this foul-mouthed Marvel character. In any case, the load of the insult in the ST has been maintained in the TT.

Exercise 4.24

Once Upon a Time in Hollywood – DVD version
Context: Pussycat, a young hippy girl, is on the street and insults a police officer when she sees him in a car.
ST: **Fuck you**, you **fucking pig**.
TT: ¡Que te den, **cerdo de mierda**!   [Get given (Fuck you), shitty pig!]
Category/subcategory: Offensive/swear word   Strategy/technique: Reformulation/Transfer (toned down)   Category/subcategory: Offensive/insult   Strategy/technique: Substitution/Transfer (load maintained)

This example contains two cases under analysis. First, the derogatory phrase 'Fuck you' has been softened with the Spanish expression *Que te den* [Get given (Fuck you)], a euphemistic formula to avoid the use of 'fuck you'. However, the transfer has been made. Second, there is an insult in the form of 'fucking pig', translated idiomatically as *cerdo de mierda* [shitty pig], which preserves the tone of the original. It is not always easy to include all offensive or taboo elements an utterance has in a subtitle, but the subtitler has been able to do so.

Exercise 4.25

Knives Out – Netflix
Context: Harlan Thrombey, renowned crime novelist, is found dead. When his family is told that Marta Cabrera is inheriting Harlan Thrombey's fortune, grandson Jacob Thrombey insults her.
ST: You **had sex** with my grandpa, you **dirty anchor baby**?
TT: ¡**Te acostabas** con mi abuelo, **panchita pervertida**!   [**You were sleeping** with my grandfather, **panchita pervert**!]
Category/subcategory: Taboo/sex   Strategy/technique: Reformulation/Transfer (load toned down)   Category/subcategory: Offensive/insult   Strategy/technique: Substitution/Transfer (load maintained)

Two cases are under analysis in this example. First, 'had sex' has been toned down with the euphemism *Te acostabas* [You were sleeping]. However, the transfer has been made possible. Second, the insult, 'dirty anchor baby', refers to someone who has obtained citizenship of the country where he/she was born, but whose parents are illegal citizens in that country. It has been substituted with a term which is perfectly understood by the target audience, *panchita* [panchita], a derogatory term used to refer to Latin Americans living in Spain. Albeit the first case was toned down, the second case maintains the load of the original, providing the subtitle with a strong racist tone.

Exercise 4.26

Snatch – DVD version
Context: Turco and Tommy are trying to do business with Micky, the leader of a family of gypsies, and is offered a caravan with no wheels as part of their deal.
ST: Why **the fuck** do I want a caravan that's got no **fucking** wheels?
TT: ¿Para qué quiero una caravana sin ruedas? [What do I want a caravan without wheels for?]
Category/subcategory: Offensive/swear word Strategy/technique: Omission/Non-transfer (load omitted)
Category/subcategory: Offensive/swear word Strategy/technique: Omission/Non-transfer (load omitted)

This example contains two swear words: 'the fuck' and 'fucking'. Because of the speaker's speed when talking and the density of words in the ST, the subtitler was probably forced to omit both elements in the subtitle. As we have already discussed, abiding by spatiotemporal restrictions prevails over the transfer of offensive and taboo elements.

Exercise 4.27

Deadpool 2 – DVD version
Context: A criminal asks for help as Deadpool is preparing to kill him.
ST: Hurry up and open this **fucking** door, and **let's kill** this **motherfucker**.
TT: ¡Ábreme, **joder**! ¡**Hay que matar** a este **hijoputa**! [Open me, **fuck**! **We have to kill** this **motherfucker**!]
Category/subcategory: Offensive/swear word Strategy/technique: Substitution/Transfer (load maintained)
Category/subcategory: Offensive/threat *and* insult Strategy/technique: Literal translation/Transfer (load maintained)

First, the offensive term 'fucking' has been substituted with *joder* [fuck]. Thus, the load of the ST has been transferred to the TT. Second, the threat phrase 'We have to kill' and the insult 'motherfucker' can be said to have been translated literally, as ¡*Hay que matar a este hijoputa*! [We have to kill this motherfucker!], which is the fusion of *hijo de puta* [son of bitch]. It must be said that although *hijoputa* is very colloquial, it is very much used in oral language and is often employed in subtitling because of the use of fewer characters.

Exercise 4.28

Pulp Fiction – DVD version
Context: Mia, thinking she is going to inhale cocaine, takes an overdose of Vince's heroin powder. Vince tries to save her life with Lance, his drug dealer's help.
ST: What **the hell** was that?
TT: ¿Qué **coño** ha sido eso? [What **the fuck** has that been?]
Category/subcategory: Offensive/swear word Strategy/technique: Substitution/Transfer (load toned up)

This example shows a case in which the offensive phrase is mild, but gets stronger in the TT through substitution. 'What the hell' has been subtitled as *Qué coño* [What the fuck]. Thus, the subtitler has probably emphasised the character's offensive way of talking throughout the film.

Exercise 4.29

Deadpool 2 – DVD version
Context: Firefist talks to Deadpool on the street damaged by the fire the former has made. After Firefist attacks Colossus with a fire ball, Deadpool reacts.
ST: Oh, **shit**! That **fucking** does it!
TT: ¡**Joder**, ahora sí que **la has cagado**! [**Fuck**, now **you really have shitted on it (screwed it up)**!]
Category/subcategory: Offensive/expletive *or* Taboo/scatology Strategy/technique: Substitution/Transfer (load maintained)
Category/subcategory: Offensive/swear word Strategy/technique: Reformulation/Transfer (load maintained)

In the first case, the term 'shit' has been substituted with *Joder* [Fuck], transferring the tone of the ST. As for the second, the phrase that includes 'fucking' has been reformulated idiomatically via *la has cagado* [you really have shitted on it (screwed it up!)]. In both cases, the taboo and offensive load has been transferred through offensive and taboo elements, that is, the categories used in the TT have been reversed.

Exercise 4.30

Snatch – DVD version

Context: Bullet-Tooth Tony is being held at gunpoint by Sol and his pals. Bullet-Tooth-Tony challenges them with his daring words.

ST: There are two types of **balls**: there are **big brave balls**, and there are **little faggot balls**.

TT:
> Hay dos tipos de **pelotas**:
> [There are two types of **balls**:]
>
> **Pelotas de machote**
> y **pelotas de maricón**.
> [**Balls of badass**
> and **balls of faggot**.]

Category/subcategory: Taboo/sex
Strategy/technique: Literal translation/Transfer (load maintained)

Category/subcategory: Taboo/sex
Strategy/technique: Literal translation/Transfer (load maintained)

Category/subcategory: Taboo/sex
Strategy/technique: Literal translation/Transfer (load maintained)

This example contains the euphemistic word for bollocks in the form of 'balls'. All these terms have been subtitled in a faithful way. We can observe that the phrase referring to heterosexuals, *Pelotas de machote* [Balls of badass], does not aim to offend the viewers, but when using the term 'faggot', we notice the homophobic tone which gets transferred to the TT with *pelotas de maricón* [balls of faggot]. In any case, the subtitler has been faithful to the original which contains a hateful tone towards the gay and bisexual community.

Exercise 4.31

Once Upon a Time in Hollywood – DVD version

Context: Rick Dalton is in his wagon and does not stop swearing and talking to himself because of his bad acting performance.

ST: You're **a fucking miserable drunk**.

TT:
> ¡Eres **un borracho de mierda**!
> [You are **a drunk piece of shit**!]

Category/subcategory: Taboo/alcohol consumption *or* Offensive/insult
Strategy/technique: Reformulation/Transfer (load maintained)

In this subtitle, we can see the phrase 'a fucking miserable drunk', which is taboo as it concerns alcohol consumption. It could also be considered an insult, despite the fact that the speaker is talking to himself. The reformulation strategy has been used as there has been a condensation of 'fucking miserable drunk' into *un borracho de mierda* [a drunk piece of shit]. The transfer of the load has been maintained.

Exercise 4.32

Deadpool 2 – DVD version
Context: Firefist has damaged the street with fire and is surrounded by the police. He challenges everyone looking at him.
ST: Do you wanna fucking die?
TT: ¿Queréis morir, cabrones?   [Do you want to die, bastards?]
Category/subcategory: Offensive/threat Strategy/technique: Substitution/Transfer (load toned up)

In this example, there is a threat in the form of the killing/violence offensive phrase 'Do you wanna [..] die?', which is intensified by the word 'fucking'. The subtitler has toned up the TT with the addition of the insult *cabrones* [bastards]. This element placed at the end of the question allows for the whole transfer of the load of the original to the subtitle.

Exercise 4.33

Nine Perfect Strangers SE01 EP04 – Prime Video
Context: Nine strangers gather at a retreat in a health-and-wellness resort. Masha Dmitrichenko, the guru, tells the group that they have been micro dosed with the drug psilocybin. Tony Hogburn complains to her after hearing this.
ST: God, you got some balls shaming me about some wine and a couple of Kit Kats. All the while, **you're dosing us with psychedelics**?

TT: **Hay que tener morro** para echarme en cara
       un poco de vino y un par de Kit-Kats
       [**You have a real nerve** to throw in my face
       a bit of wine and a couple of Kit Kats.]
 	
       mientras tú **nos metes drogas psicodélicas**.
       [while **you are putting psychedelic drugs on us**.]

Category/subcategory: Taboo/profanity Strategy/technique: Omission/Non-transfer (load omitted) Category/subcategory: Taboo/sex Strategy/technique: Reformulation/Transfer (load toned down) Category/subcategory: Taboo/drugs consumption Strategy/technique: Reformulation/Transfer (load maintained)

Three cases are under analysis in these subtitles. First, the script is wordy and the religious reference to 'God' has been omitted, probably because of the challenge of including so much information in the two subtitles. Thus, the transfer has not been made. Second, the speaker says 'you got some balls' which is a male reference even though it is addressed to a female character. The transfer has been toned down with a more neutral phrase as *Hay que tener morro* [You have a real nerve]. However, we can argue that there has been a transfer of the load. Third, there is an allusion to getting drugged by another person with the question 'you're dosing us with psychedelics?'. It has been reformulated as the ST has two different sentences, the second being a question, and both of them are shown in two subtitles as a single compound sentence. The transfer has been made as we can see in *nos metes drogas psicodélicas* [you are putting psychedelic drugs on us.]. These cases serve as an example to reinforce the idea that subtitling is characterised by condensation of the original script.

Exercise 4.34

Django Unchained – Netflix
Context: Django shoots Stephen in the kneecap and the latter insults him.
ST: Oh, sweet Jesus, let me **kill** this **"n****r"**.
TT: ¡Dios santo, déjame **matar** a este **negro**! [God saint, let me **kill** this **black**!]
Category/subcategory: Offensive/violence Strategy/technique: Literal translation/Transfer (load maintained)
Category/subcategory: Offensive swearing/insult Strategy/technique: Substitution/Transfer (load toned down)

In the first place, 'sweet Jesus' could not be considered offensive because of the adjective employed, that is, 'sweet'. However, then we can look into two cases. First, the killing-related verb 'kill' has been transferred in literal terms as *matar* [kill]. The transfer has therefore been made. Second, the insult 'n****r' has been substituted with *negro* [black]. Albeit, addressing someone by the colour of his/her skin can be considered racist, the strength the word 'n****r' has in the ST gets softened in the TT. We can argue that the transfer has been made, but without the same racist tone. In addition, audiovisual translators need to be consistent in cases like this in which the same term with such a strong load needs to be translated in a similar way across the subtitles so that the audience does not get confused with the terminological variety.

Exercise 4.35

Knives Out – Netflix
Context: Harlan Thrombey, renowned crime novelist, is found dead. When his family is told that Marta Cabrera is inheriting Harlan Thrombey's fortune, Linda Drysdale starts asking Marta disrespectful questions in anger.
ST: What were you doing? **Were you boinking** my father?
TT: ¿Qué hacías? ¿El **ñiqui-ñinqui** con mi padre? [What were you doing? **Rumpy-pumpy** with my dad?]
Category/subcategory: Taboo/sex Strategy/technique: Lexical recreation/Transfer (load maintained)

The verb 'boinking' in the subtitle refers to having sex and has been transferred to the TT through lexical recreation. The chosen slang word is *ñiqui-ñinqui*, although an expression more usually used is *ñaca-ñaca* (rumpy-pumpy), a euphemism to avoid the use of the verbs 'fuck' or even 'have sex'. We could think that the subtitler has aimed to adapt the latter expression with a touch of humour, which is in line with the genre of the film.

Exercise 4.36

Once Upon a Time in Hollywood – DVD version
Context: Rick Dalton is in his wagon and does not stop swearing and talking to himself because of his bad acting performance.
ST: **Fucking damn it**, Rick, **I swear to God**. Forgot your **fucking** lines,
TT: ¡**Me cago en la puta**, Rick!   ¡Has olvidado el **puto** texto!   [I shit on the whore (Fucking hell), Rick!   You have forgotten the **fucking** text!]
Category/subcategory: Offensive/curse   Strategy/technique: Reformulation/Transfer (load maintained)   Category/subcategory: Offensive/swearing   Strategy/technique: Omission/Non-transfer (load omitted)   Category/subcategory: Offensive/swear word   Strategy/technique: Literal translation/Transfer (load maintained)

In this example, we can observe three cases under analysis in a scene in which the character is talking to himself rather quickly. First, the curse 'Fucking damn it' has been reformulated in similar terms as *¡Me cago en la puta!* [I shit on the whore (Fucking hell)]. Accordingly, the transfer has been possible. Second, the swearing 'I swear to God' has been omitted in the subtitle probably due to the spatiotemporal constraints of the subtitle. Third, the swear word 'fucking' has been translated literally in the TT. This is another example of the difficulties of subtitling consecutive dialogue exchanges full of swearing. Not all of them would usually be prone to transfer.

Exercise 4.37

Nine Perfect Strangers SE01 EP07 – Prime Video
Context: Nine strangers gather at a retreat in a health-and-wellness resort. Masha Dmitrichenko has a conversation with Carmel Schneider and the latter starts talking to her aggressively.
ST: My daughters. You **fucking bitch**, they're my daughters, Lillian! **I fucking hate you**.
TT: Son mis hijas, ¡**puta de mierda**!   ¡Son mis hijas, Lillian! ¡**Te odio, joder**!   [They are my daughters, **shitty whore**!   They are my daughters, Lillian! **I hate you, fuck**!]
Category/subcategory: Offensive/insult   Strategy/technique: Substitution/Transfer (load maintained)   Category/subcategory: Offensive/violence   Strategy/technique: Reformulation/Transfer (load maintained)

This example has two cases. In the first place, the insult 'fucking bitch' has been substituted with *puta de mierda* [shitty whore]. This rendering transmits the same offensive load for which reason the transfer has been made. In the second place, we can argue that 'I fucking hate you' is an offensive expression, as it concerns verbal violence given that the character is expressing her feelings of hate towards another woman. In addition, this statement is reinforced by the term 'fucking'. Its reformulation as *¡Te odio, joder!* [I hate you, fuck] allows the subtitler to transmit all the load of the ST exchange to the TT.

Exercise 4.38

Fleabag SE01 EP01– Prime Video
Context: Fleabag is having sex with her hookup Arsehole Guy, while narrating to the audience what is to come.
ST: After some pretty standard **bouncing**, you realise **he's edging towards your asshole**.
TT: Después de un rato de **folleteo** estándar, [After a while of standard **screwing**,] te das cuenta de que **se está dirigiendo a tu agujero del culo**. [you realised that **he is pointing at your hole in the ass**.]
Category/subcategory: Taboo/sex Strategy/technique: Lexical recreation/Transfer (load maintained)
Category/subcategory: Taboo/sex Strategy/technique: Literal translation/Transfer (load maintained)

The visual channel allows the audience to see that a couple is having sex and the woman is saying this to the camera as a narrator. This visual information is of great help to audiovisual translators because of the information shown on the screen, avoiding unnecessary linguistic elements in the TT. In the first subtitle, the verb 'bouncing' refers in this case to having sex, which has been translated via lexical recreation with the word *folleteo* [screwing]. This Spanish term can be understood perfectly well by the audience, and although it is not a term considered by the RAE [Spanish Royal Academy], it does transfer the sexual connotation of the ST. In the second subtitle, the term 'penis' is not mentioned, but through the context it can be inferred that the character is talking about it in order to have anal sex. The expression 'he's edging towards your asshole' has been translated in very similar terms as *se está dirigiendo a tu agujero del culo* [he is pointing at your hole in the ass]. Thus, the transfer has also been possible.

Exercise 4.39

Nine Perfect Strangers SE01 EP01 – Prime Video

Context: Nine strangers gather at a retreat in a health-and-wellness resort. Frances Welty receives a phone call with bad news, so she starts releasing her anger by talking to herself.

ST: Dead to the **fucking** world.

TT:
>¡Muerta para el **puto** mundo!
>[Dead to the **fucking** world!]

Category/subcategory: Offensive/swear word
Strategy/technique: Literal translation/Transfer (load maintained)

The term 'Dead' in this scene means to be finished, which is the reason why it is not considered within the scope of this analysis. As for the use of the swear word 'fucking', it has been very closely subtitled. In this case, the subtitler has been able to transfer all the load the ST contains to the TT.

Exercise 4.40

Fleabag SE02 EP05 – Prime Video

Context: Fleabag is in her shop. Her ex brother-in-law, Martin, pays her a visit. They start arguing and then move on to insulting each other.

ST: -I will take you down, **fucker**. -I will take you down, **fucker**. -No. -**Fuck you**! -**Fuck you**!

TT:
>**Voy a hundirte, zorra.**
>[I am going to take you down, bitch.]
>
>-Lo mismo te digo, **cabrón**.
>-No.
>[I tell you the same, **fucker**.
>-No.]
>
>-¡**Que te follen**!
>-¡**Que te follen**!
>[-**Fuck you**!
>-**Fuck you**!]

Category/subcategory: Offensive/violence
Strategy/technique: Reformulation/Transfer (load maintained) (x2)

Category/subcategory: Offensive/insult
Strategy/technique: Substitution/Transfer(load toned up)

Category/subcategory: Offensive/insult
Strategy/technique: Literal translation/Transfer (load maintained)

Category/subcategory: Taboo/sex
Strategy/technique: Literal translation/Transfer (load maintained) (x2)

These three subtitles are full of offensive and taboo content. In the first subtitle, there is a verbal violence-related phrase uttered later by the other speaker, 'I will take you down'. This has been reformulated as *Voy a hundirte* [I am going to take you down]. In the second subtitle, it has been reformulated with different words as *Lo mismo te digo* [I tell you the same], to avoid being repetitive. In both cases, the transfer has been made. As for the insult 'fucker' in the first subtitle, which was addressed to the woman in the scene, it has been substituted with *zorra* [bitch], whose tone has been toned up. In the second case, 'fucker', which was addressed to the man in the scene, has been translated literally as *cabrón* [fucker], for which reason the transfer has been maintained. In the third subtitle, both characters utter 'Fuck you!', which gets similarly translated as *¡Que te follen*! [Fuck you!]. Once again, the transfer has been made possible and with the aim of consistency the subtitler has employed similar vulgar phrases for the TT.

Note

(1) Retrieved from https://www.etymonline.com/search?q=boche.

References

Al-Adwan, A.S. (2015) Towards a model of euphemisation in Arabic subtitling. *Arab World English Journal (AWEJ) Special Issue on Translation* 4, 6–21.

Allan, K. and Burridge, K. (1991) *Euphemism and Dysphemism: Language Used as Shield and Weapon*. Oxford: Oxford University Press.

Allan, K. and Burridge, K. (2006) *Forbidden Words: Taboo and the Censoring of Language*. Cambridge: Cambridge University Press.

Allen, I.L. (1983) *The Language of Ethnic Conflict: Social Organization and Lexical Culture*. New York: Columbia University Press.

Alsharhan, A. (2020) Netflix no-censorship policy in subtitling taboo language from English into Arabic. *JAT: Journal of Audiovisual Translation* 3 (1), 7–28.

Andersson, L.-G. and Trudgill, P. (1990) *Bad Language*. Oxford: Basil Blackwell.

Ávila, A. (1997) *La censura del doblaje cinematográfico en España*. Barcelona: CIMS, Libros de Comunicación Global.

Ávila-Cabrera, J.J. (2013) Subtitling multilingual films: The case of *Inglourious Basterds*. *RAEL: Revista Electrónica de Lingüística Aplicada* 12, 87–100.

Ávila-Cabrera, J.J. (2014) The subtitling of offensive and taboo language: A descriptive study. PhD thesis, Universidad Nacional de Educación a Distancia.

Ávila-Cabrera, J.J. (2015a) An account of the subtitling of offensive and taboo language in Tarantino's screenplays. *Sendebar* 26, 37–56.

Ávila-Cabrera, J.J. (2015b) Propuesta de modelo de análisis del lenguaje ofensivo y tabú en la subtitulación. *Verbeia: Revista de estudios filológicos*, 8–27.

Ávila-Cabrera, J.J. (2015c) Subtitling Tarantino's offensive and taboo dialogue exchanges into European Spanish: The case of *Pulp Fiction*. *Revista de Lingüística y Lenguas Aplicadas* 10, 1–11.

Ávila-Cabrera, J.J. (2016a) The subtitling of offensive and taboo language into Spanish of *Inglourious Basterds*: A case study. *Babel: Revue Internationale de la Traduction* 62 (2), 211–232.

Ávila-Cabrera, J.J. (2016b) The treatment of offensive and taboo language in the subtitling of *Reservoir Dogs* into Spanish. *TRANS: Revista de Traductología* 20, 25–40.

Ávila-Cabrera, J.J. (2017) La subtitulación del lenguaje ofensivo y tabú. Estudio descriptivo. In J.J. Martínez Sierra (coord.) *Fotografía de la investigación doctoral en traducción audiovisual* (vol. 2, pp. 13–31). Madrid: Bohodón Ediciones.

Ávila-Cabrera, J.J. (2020) Profanity and blasphemy in the subtitling of English into European Spanish: Four case studies based on a selection of Tarantino's films. *Quaderns. Revista de Traducció* 27, 125–141.

Ávila-Cabrera, J.J. and Rodríguez Arancón, P. (2018) The OffTaTled project: OFFensive and TAboo Exchanges SubtiTLED by online university students. *Encuentro: Revista de Investigación e Innovación en la clase de idiomas* 27, 204–219.

Azzaro, G. (2005) *Four-Letter Films: Taboo Language in Movies*. Rome: Aracne.

Baker, M. and Hochel, B. (1998) Dubbing. In M. Baker (ed.) *Routledge Encyclopedia of Translation Studies* (pp. 74–76). London: Routledge.

Baldry, A. and Thibault, P.J. (2006) *Multimodal Transcription and Text Analysis: A Multimedia Toolkit and Coursebook*. London: Equinox.

Bandín Fuertes, E. (2011) Performing Shakespeare in a conflicting cultural context: Othello in Francoist Spain. *Sederi* 21, 119–132.

Bogucki, L. and Deckert, M. (eds) (2020) *The Palgrave Handbook of Audiovisual Translation and Media Accessibility*. Cham: Palgrave Macmillan.

Bolaños García Escribano, A. (2017) La variación lingüística en subtitulación: El caso de las restricciones en los Amores imaginarios de Xavier Dolan. *Entreculturas 9*, 221–237.

Bolaños-García-Escribano, A., Díaz Cintas, J. and Massidda, S. (2021) Subtitlers on the Cloud: The use of professional web-based systems in subtitling practice and training. *Revista Tradumàtica: Tecnologies de la Traducció* 19, 1–21.

Borrás, I. and Lafayette, R.C. (1994) Effects of multimedia courseware subtitling on the speaking performance of college students of French. *Modern Language Journal* 78 (1), 61–75.

Botella Tejera, C. (2018) La traducción del humor intertextual audiovisual. Que la fuerza os acompañe. *MonTI: Monografías De Traducción E Interpretación* 9, 77–100.

Bravo, J.M. (2004) Conventional subtitling, screen texts and film titles. In J.M. Bravo (ed.) *A New Spectrum of Translation Studies* (pp. 208–230). Valladolid: Universidad de Valladolid.

Brondeel, H. (1994) Teaching subtitling routines. *Meta* 34 (1), 26–33.

Bucaria, C. (2017) Genetically modified TV, or the manipulation of US television series in Italy. *Perspectives* 26 (6), 930–945.

Chaume, F. (2000) La traducción audiovisual: Estudio descriptivo y modelo de análisis de los textos audiovisuales para su traducción. PhD thesis, Universitat Jaume I.

Chaume, F. (2004a) Discourse markers in audiovisual translation. *Meta* 49 (4), 843–855.

Chaume, F. (2004b) Film studies and translation studies: Two disciplines at a stake in audiovisual translation. *Meta* 49 (1), 12–24.

Chaume, F. (2018) Is audiovisual translation putting the concept of translation up against the ropes? *JoSTrans: Journal of Specialised Translation* 30, 84–104.

Chiaro, D. (2018) *The Language of Jokes in the Digital Age*. Abingdon: Routledge.

Corral Esteban, A. (2019) Metaphor and linguistic diversity. Presentation at the conference The Creative Power of Metaphor, University of Oxford, Oxford, 29–30 March.

Culpeper, J. (2005) Impoliteness and entertainment in the television quiz show: The Weakest Link. *Journal of Politeness Research* 1, 35–72.

Creswell, J.W. (2003) *Research Design: Qualitative, Quantitative, and Mixed Methods Approaches* (2nd edn). Thousand Oaks, CA: Sage.

Dalzell, T. and Victor, T. (2008) *The Concise New Partridge Dictionary of Slang and Unconventional English* (8th edn). New York: Routledge.

Danan, M. (1991) Dubbing as an expression of nationalism. *Meta* 36 (4), 606–614.

De Higes-Andino, I. (2014) The translation of multilingual films: Modes, strategies, constraints and manipulation in the Spanish translations of It's a Free World... *Linguistica Antverpiensia, New Series – Themes in Translation Studies* 13, 211–231.

Delabastita, D. (1989) Translation and mass-communication: Film and TV translation as evidence of cultural dynamics. *Babel: Revue Internationale de la Traduction* 35 (4), 193–218.

Delabastita, D. (2014) Introduction. *The Translator* 2 (2), 127–139.

Díaz Cintas, J. (1997) El subtitulado en tanto que modalidad de traducción fílmica dentro del marco teórico de los Estudios sobre Traducción. (Misterioso asesinato en *Manhattan*, Woody Allen, 1993). PhD thesis, Universitat de València.

Díaz Cintas, J. (2001a) *La traducción audiovisual: el subtitulado*. Salamanca: Almar.

Díaz Cintas, J. (2001b) Sex, (sub)titles and videotapes. In L. Lorenzo García and A.M. Pereira Rodríguez (eds) *Traducción subordinada II: el subtitulado (inglés – español/ galego)* (pp. 47–67). Vigo: Universidad de Vigo.

Díaz Cintas, J. (ed.) (2008) *The Didactics of Audiovisual Translation*. Amsterdam: John Benjamins.

Díaz Cintas, J. (2009) Introduction - Audiovisual translation: An overview of its potential. In J. Díaz Cintas (ed.) *New Trends in Audiovisual Translation* (pp. 1–18). Bristol: Multilingual Matters.

Díaz Cintas, J. (2011) Dealing with multilingual films in audiovisual translation. In W. Pöckl, I. Ohnheiser and P. Sandrini (eds) *Translation, Sprachvariation, Mehrsprachigkeit. Festschrift für Lew Zybatow zum 60. Geburtstag* (pp. 215–233). Frankfurt am Main: Peter Lang.

Díaz Cintas, J. (2012) Clearing the smoke to see the screen: Ideological manipulation in audiovisual translation. *Meta* 57 (2), 279–293.

Díaz Cintas, J. (2018) Subtitling's a carnival: New practices in cyberspace. *JoSTrans: Journal of Specialised Translation* 30, 127–149.

Díaz Cintas, J. (2019) Film censorship in Franco's Spain: The transforming power of dubbing. *Perspectives* 27 (2), 182–200.

Díaz Cintas, J. and Remael, A. (2007) *Audiovisual Translation: Subtitling*. Manchester: St Jerome.

Díaz Cintas, J. and Anderman, G. (ed.) (2009) *Audiovisual Translation: Language Transfer on Screen*. Basingstoke: Palgrave Macmillan.

Díaz Cintas, J. and Remael, A. (2021) *Subtitling: Concepts and Practices*. New York: Routledge.

Dore, M. (2019) Multilingual humour in audiovisual translation. *Modern Family* dubbed in Italian. *The European Journal of Humour Research* 7 (1), 52–70.

d'Ydewalle, G., Van Rensbergen, J. and Pollet, J. (1987) Reading a message when the same message is available auditorily in another language: The case of subtitling. In J.K. O'Regan and A. Lévy-Schoen (eds) *Eye Movements: From Physiology to Cognition* (pp. 313–321). Amsterdam: Elsevier Science Publishers.

Eguíluz, F., Merino, R., Olsen, V., Pajares, E. and Santamaría, J.M. (eds) (1994) *Transvases culturales: literatura, cine, traducción*. Vitoria-Gasteiz: Universidad del País Vasco.

Fernández Dobao, A.M. (2006) Linguistic and cultural aspects of the translation of swearing: The Spanish version of *Pulp Fiction. Babel* 52 (3), 222–242.

Filmer, D. (2012) The 'gook' goes 'gay'. Cultural interference in translating offensive language. *Intralinea* 15.

Fodor, I. (1976) *Film Dubbing: Phonetic, Semiotic, Esthetic and Psychological Aspects*. Hamburg: Buske.

Fuentes-Luque, A. (2015) El lenguaje tabú en la traducción audiovisual: Límites lingüísticos, culturales y sociales. *E-AESLA* 1.

Gambier, Y. (1994) Audio-visual communication: Typological detour. In C. Dollerup and A. Loddegaard (eds) *Teaching Translation and Interpreting 2* (pp. 275–283). Amsterdam: John Benjamins.

Gambier, Y. and Gottlieb, H. (eds) (2001) *(Multi)Media Translation*. Amsterdam: John Benjamins.

Gentzler, E. (2004) *Contemporary Translation Theories*. Shanghai: Shanghai Foreign Language Education Press.

Godayol, P. (2020) "Un espacio de trabajo en relación": El ensayo feminista traducido de Lasal, Edicions de les dones. *"Transfer" XV* 1-2, 115–141.

Gómez Castro, C. (2020) Harold Robbins' *The Betsy* and its Spanish translation. *Translation Matters* 2 (2), 97–112.

Gonzalez Vera, P. (2015) When humour gets fishy: The translation of humour in animated films. In J. Díaz Cintas and J. Neves (eds) *Audiovisual Translation: Taking Stock* (pp. 123–139). Newcastle upon Tyne: Cambridge Scholars Publishing.

Gottlieb, H. (2010) Subtitling: Diagonal translation. *Perspectives: Studies in Translatology* 2 (1), 101–121.
Guillot, M-N. (2019) Subtitling's cross-cultural expressivity put to the test: A cross-sectional study of linguistic and cultural representation across Romance and Germanic language. *Multilingua* 38 (5), 505–528.
Guillot, M-N. (2020) The pragmatics of audiovisual translation: Voices from within in film subtitling. *Journal of Pragmatics* 170, 317–330.
Gubern, R. (1981) *La censura. Función política y ordenamiento jurídico bajo el Franquismo 1936–1975*. Barcelona: Península.
Gubern, R. and Font, D. (1975) *Un cine para el cadalso. 40 años de censura cinematográfica en España*. Barcelona: Euros.
Gutiérrez Lanza, C. (1999) Traducción y censura de textos cinematográficos en la España de Franco: Doblaje y subtitulado inglés-español (1951–1975). PhD thesis, Universidad de León.
Gutiérrez Lanza, C. (2007) Traducción inglés-español y censura de textos cinematográficos: Definición, construcción y análisis del corpus 0/Catálogo TRACEci (1951–1981). In R. Merino Álvarez (ed.) *Traducción y censura en España (1939–1985). Estudios sobre corpus TRACE: cine, narrativa, teatro* (pp. 197–240). Bilbao: Universidad del País Vasco.
Gutiérrez Lanza, C. (2011) Censors and censorship boards in Franco's Spain (1950s–1960s): An overview based on the TRACE cinema catalogue. In D. Asimakoulas and M. Rogers (eds) *Translation and Opposition* (pp. 305–320). Bristol: Multilingual Matters.
Hatim, B. and Mason, I. (1997) *The Translator as Communicator*. New York: Routledge.
Hughes, G. (2006) *An Encyclopedia of Swearing: The Social History of Oaths, Profanity, Foul Language, and Ethnic Slurs in the English-Speaking World*. London: M.E. Sharpe.
Hurtado Albir, A. (1999) *Enseñar a traducir*. Madrid: Edelsa.
Ivarsson, J. and Carroll, M. (1998) *Subtitling*. Simrishamn: TransEdit.
Izwaini, S. (2017b) Translation of taboo expressions in Arabic subtitling. In A. Baczkowska (ed.) *Interfaces, Impoliteness in Media Discourse* (pp. 149–161). Frankfurt am Main: Peter Lang.
Izwaini, S. (2018) Censorship and manipulation of subtitling in the Arab world. In J. Díaz Cintas and K. Nikolić (eds) *Fast-Forwarding with Audiovisual Translation* (pp. 47–57). Bristol: Multilingual Matters.
Jay, T.B. (1980) Sex roles and dirty word usage: A review of the literature and a reply to Haas. *Psychological Bulletin* 88 (3), 614–621.
Jay, T.B. (1992) *Cursing in America: A Psycholinguistic Study of Dirty Language in the Courts, in the Movies, in the Schoolyards, and on the Streets*. Amsterdam: John Benjamins.
Jay, T.B. (2000) *Why We Curse*. Philadelphia, PA: John Benjamins.
Jay, T.B. (2009) The utility and ubiquity of taboo words. *Perspectives on Psychological Science* 4 (2), 153–161.
Jay, T.B. and Janschewitz, K. (2008) *The Pragmatics of Swearing*. Berlin: Walter de Gruyter.
Khoshsaligheh, M., Ameri, S. and Mehdizadkhani, M. (2018) A sociocultural study of taboo rendition in Persian fansubbing: An issue of resistance. *Language and Intercultural Communication* 18 (6), 663–680.
Lambert, W.E., Boehler, I. and Sidoti, N. (1981) Choosing the languages of subtitles and spoken dialogues for media presentations: Implications for second language education. *Applied Psycholinguistics* 2 (2), 133–148.
Lecuona Lerchundi, L. (1994) Entre el doblaje y la subtitulación: La interpretación simultánea en el cine. In F. Eguíluz, R. Merino, V. Olsen, E. Pajares and M. Santamaría (eds) *Transvases culturales: Literatura, cine, traducción* (pp. 279–286). Vitoria-Gasteiz: Universidad del País Vasco.

Lefevere, A. (1992) *Translation, Rewriting, and the Manipulation of Literary Fame*. New York: Routledge.
Legido, R. (2021) *Escondidas en el cine. Censura y personajes sáficos*. Murcia: Letras raras ediciones, S.L.U.
Levinson, S.C. (1983) *Pragmatics*. Cambridge: Cambridge University Press.
Lobejón Santos, S. (2013) Traducción y censura de texos poéticos inglés-español en España: TRACEpi (1939–1983). PhD thesis, Universidad de León.
Lung, R. (1998) On mis-translating sexually suggestive elements in English-Chinese screen subtitling. *Babel: Revue Internationale de la Traduction* 44 (2), 97–109.
Luyken, G-M., Herbst, T., Langham-Brown, J., Reid, H. and Spinhof, H. (eds) (1991) *Overcoming Language Barriers in Television: Dubbing and Subtitling for the European Audience*. Manchester: European Institute for the Media.
Martínez Pleguezuelos, A.J. (2021) Translating the gay identity in audiovisual media. The case of *Will and Grace*. *Spanish Journal of Applied Linguistics* 34 (1), 201–225.
Martínez Sierra, J.J. (2006) Translating audiovisual humour. A case study. *Perspectives: Studies in Translatology* 13 (4), 289–296.
Martínez Sierra, J.J. (2017) Dealing with the n-word in dubbing and subtitling *Django Unchained*: A case of self-censorship? *Ideas* (3) 3, 39–56.
Martínez Sierra, J.J. (ed.) (2021) *Multilingualism, Translation and Language Teaching*. Valencia: Tirant Lo Blanch.
Mason, I. (1989) Speaker meaning and reader meaning: Preserving coherence in screen translation. In H. Prais, R. Kölmel and J. Payne (eds) *Babel: The Cultural and Linguistic Barriers between Nations* (pp. 13–24). Aberdeen: Aberdeen University Press.
Maxwell, J.A. (2005) *Qualitative Research Design: An Interactive Approach* (2nd edn). Thousand Oaks, CA: Sage.
Mayoral, R. (1993) La traducción cinematográfica: El subtitulado. *Sendebar* 4, 45–68.
Mayoral, R., Kelly, D. and Gallardo, N. (1988) Concept of constrained translation: Non-linguistic perspectives of translation. *Meta* 33 (3), 356–367.
McEnery, T. (2006) *Swearing in English. Bad Language, Purity and Power from 1586 to the Present*. New York: Routledge.
Merino Álvarez, R. (ed.) (2007) *Traducción y censura en España (1939–1985). Estudios sobre corpus TRACE: Cine, narrativa, teatro*. Bilbao: Universidad del País Vasco.
Molina, L. and Hurtado Albir, A. (2002) Translation techniques revisited: A dynamic and functionalist approach. *Meta* 47 (4), 498–512.
Montagu, A. (1973 [1967]) *The Anatomy of Swearing* (2nd edn). London: MacMillan.
Murray, J., Bradley, H. Craigie, W. and Onions, C. (1884) *Oxford English Dictionary*. Oxford: Oxford University Press.
Nabokov, V. (1955) *Lolita*. Penguin Modern Classics (2000) ebook.
Neves, J. (2005) Audiovisual translation: Subtitling for the deaf and hard-of-hearing. PhD thesis, Roehampton University.
Neves, J. (2009) Interlingual subtitling for the deaf and hard-of-hearing. In J. Díaz Cintas and G. Anderman (eds) *Audiovisual Translation: Language Transfer on Screen* (pp. 151–169). Basingstoke: Palgrave Macmillan.
New Oxford Dictionary of English, The (2001) Judy Pearsall (ed.) Oxford: Oxford University Press.
O'Driscoll, J. (2020) *Offensive Language. Taboo, Offence and Social Control*. London: Bloomsbury.
Orero, P. (2004) Audiovisual translation: A new dynamic umbrella. In P. Orero (ed.) *Topics in Audiovisual Translation* (pp. vii–xiii). Amsterdam: John Benjamins.
Orero, P., Pereira, A.M. and Utray, F. (2007) Visión histórica de la accesibilidad en los medios en España. *TRANS: Revista de Traductología* 11, 31–43.
Parks, C. (1994) *Closed Captioned TV: A Resource for ESL Literacy Education*. Washington, DC: ERIC Digest.

Parra López, G. (2019) Disorderly speech in audiovisual fiction and its translation: Portrayals of characters under the influence of alcohol and drugs. PhD thesis, Universitat Pompeu Fabra.

Pedersen, J. (2015) On the subtitling of visualized metaphors. *JoSTrans: The Journal of Specialised Translation* 23, 162–180.

Pérez-González, L. (2009) Audiovisual translation. In M. Baker and G. Saldanha (eds) *Routledge Enclopedia of Translation Studies* (2nd edn, pp. 13–20). New York: Routledge.

Pérez-González, L. (2014) Multimodality in translation and interpreting studies: Theoretical and methodological perspectives. In S. Bermann and C. Porter (eds) *A Companion to Translation Studies* (pp. 119–131). Chichester: Wiley-Blackwell.

Pérez L. de Heredia, M. (2014) Translating and (self) censoring for the stage or how to deal with conflict and survive. In E. Ortega Arjonilla (ed.) *Traducir la cultura: De barreras culturales en la traducción subordinada y audiovisual* (vol. 5, pp. 697–712). Granada: Comares.

Rabadán, R. (2000) *Traducción y censura inglés-español, 1939-1985: Estudio preliminar*. León: Universidad de León.

Ranzato, I. (2012) Gayspeak and gay subjects in audiovisual translation: Strategies in Italian dubbing. *Meta* 57 (2), 369–384.

Reid, H. (1978) Subtitling, the intelligent solution. In P.A. Horguelin (ed.) *Translating, a Profession. Proceedings VIII FIT World Congress* (pp. 420–428). Ottawa: Conseil des traducteurs et Interprètes du Canada.

Rioja, M. (2008) La traducción inglés-español de textos narrativos censurados (1962–1969). In L. Pérez Ruiz, I. Pizarro Sánchez and E. González-Cascos Jiménez (eds) *Estudios de Metodología de la Lengua Inglesa (IV)* (pp. 243–255). Valladolid: Universidad de Valladolid.

Roales Ruiz, A. (2014) Estudio crítico de los programas de subtitulación profesionales. Carencias en su aplicación para la didáctica. Propuesta de solución mediante conjunto de aplicaciones integradas. PhD thesis, Universidad de Salamanca.

Roales Ruiz, A. (2017) *Técnicas para la Traducción Audiovisual: Subtitulación*. Madrid: Escolar y Mayo Editores.

Roales Ruiz, A. (2018) *Didáctica de la subtitulación: Una propuesta tecnológica*. Granada: Editorial Comares.

Robson, C. (2011) *Real World Research: A Resource for Users of Social Research Methods in Applied Settings* (3rd edn). Chichester: Wiley.

Romero-Fresco, P. (2019) *Accessible Filmmaking: Integrating Translation and Accessibility into the Filmmaking Process*. New York: Routledge.

Sánchez-Mompeán, S. (2021) Netflix likes it dubbed: Taking on the challenge of dubbing into English. *Language and Communication* 80, 180–190.

Santaemilia, J. (2008) The translation of sex-related language: The danger(s) of self-censorship(s). *TTR: Traduction, Terminologie, Rédaction* 21 (2), 221–252.

Sasamoto, R., O'Hagan, M. and Doherty, S. (2017) Telop, affect, and media design: A multimodal analysis of Japanese TV programs. *Television and New Media* 18 (5), 427–440.

Scandura, G.L. (2004) Sex, lies and TV: Censorship and subtitling. *Meta* 49 (1), 125–134.

Shakespeare, W. (1991) *Othello [1622]*. Oxford: Oxford Text Archive Core Collection.

Shuttleworth, M. and Cowie, M. (1997) *Dictionary of Translation Studies*. Manchester: St. Jerome.

Snell-Hornby, M. (1988) *Translation Studies: An Integrated Approach*. Amsterdam: John Benjamins.

Sokoli, S. (2000) Research issues in audiovisual translation: Aspects of subtitling in Greece. MA dissertation, Universitat Autònoma de Barcelona.

Sokoli, S. (2006) Learning via subtitling (LvS). A tool for the creation of foreign language learning activities based on film subtitling. In M. Carroll and H. Gerzymisch-Arbogast (eds) *Proceedings of the Marie Curie Euroconferences MuTra: Audiovisual Translation Scenarios* (pp. 66–73). Copenhagen: MuTra, 1–5 May.

Sokoli, S. (2018) Exploring the possibilities of interactive audiovisual activities for language learning. *Special Issue of Translation and Translanguaging in Multilingual Contexts. Audiovisual Translation in Applied Linguistics: Beyond Case Studies* 4 (1), 77–100.

Soler Pardo, B. (2015) *On the Translation of Swearing into Spanish: From Reservoir Dogs to Inglorious Basterds*. Newcastle-upon-Tyne: Cambridge Scholars Publishing.

Spears, R.A. (2000) *NTC's Dictionary of American Slang and Colloquial Expressions*. Illinois: NTC.

Szarkowska, A. and Bogucka, L. (2019) Six-second rule revisited: An eye-tracking study on the impact of speech rate and language proficiency on subtitle reading. *Translation, Cognition & Behavior* 2 (1), 101-124.

Talaván, N. (2010) Subtitling as a task and subtitles as support: Pedagogical applications. In J. Díaz Cintas, A. Matamala and J. Neves (eds) *New Insights into Audiovisual Translation and Media Accessibility: Media for All 2* (pp. 285–299). New York: Ropodi.

Talaván, N. (2012) Justificación teórico-práctica del uso de los subtítulos en la enseñanza-aprendizaje de lenguas extranjeras. *TRANS: Revista de Traductología* 16, 23–37.

Talaván, N. (2013) *La subtitulación en el aprendizaje de lenguas extranjeras*. Barcelona: Octaedro.

Talaván, N. (2017) *Translation as a Science and Translation as an Art. A Practical Approach*. Madrid: McGraw Hill Education.

Talaván, N. (2020) The didactic value of AVT in foreign language education. In L. Bogucki and M. Deckert (eds) *The Palgrave Handbook of Audiovisual Translation and Media Accessibility* (pp. 567–591). Cham: Palgrave Macmillan.

Talaván, N. and Lertola, J. (2022) Audiovisual translation as a didactic resource in foreign language education. A methodological proposal. *Encuentro: Revista de Investigación e Innovación en la clase de idiomas* 30, 23–39.

Talaván, N., Ávila-Cabrera, J.J. and Costal, T. (2016) *Traducción y accesibilidad audiovisual*. Barcelona: Editorial UOC.

Tamayo Masero, A. and Manterola Agirrezabalaga, E. (2019) La creación, la traducción y el tratamiento lingüístico en Handi. *Hikma* 18 (1), 283–314.

Titford, C. (1982) Sub-titling: Constrained translation. *Lebende Sprachen* 27 (3), 113–116.

Toury, G. (2012) *Descriptive Translation Studies and Beyond*. Amsterdam: John Benjamins.

Valdeón, R.A. (2000) Transgressions in the foreign language: Taboo subjects, offensive language and euphemisms for Spanish learners of English. *BABEL-AFIAL* 9, 25–62.

Valdeón, R.A. (2015) The (ab)use of taboo lexis in audiovisual translation: Raising awareness of pragmatic variation in English-Spanish. *Intercultural Pragmatics* 12 (3), 363–385.

Valdeón, R.A. (2020) Swearing and the vulgarization hypothesis in Spanish audiovisual translation. *Journal of Pragmatics* 155, 261–272.

Vinay, J-P. and Dalbernet, J. (1995 [1958]) *Comparative Stylistics of French and English: A Methodology for Translation* (trans. J.C. Sager and M.J. Hamel). Amsterdam: John Benjamins.

Wajnryb, R. (2005) *Expletive Deleted: A Good Look at Bad Language*. New York: Free Press.

Xavier, C. (2021) On norms and taboo: An analysis of professional subtitling through data triangulation. *Target: International Journal of Translation Studies* 34 (1), 67–97.

Zabalbeascoa, P. (1997) Dubbing and the nonverbal dimension of translation. In F. Poyatos (ed.) *Nonverbal Communication and Translation* (pp. 327–342). Amsterdam: John Benjamins.

Zabalbeascoa, P. (2005) Humor and translation: An interdiscipline. *Humor* 18 (2), 185–207.
Zabalbeascoa, P. (2008) The nature of the audiovisual text and its parameters. In J. Díaz Cintas (ed.) *The Didactics of Audiovisual Translation* (pp. 21–38). Amsterdam: John Benjamins.
Zabalbeascoa, P. (2016) Censoring Lolita's sense of humor: When translation affects the audience's perception. *Perspectives* 24 (1), 93–114.
Zabalbeascoa, P. (2020) Multilingual humour in audiovisual translation. Multilingual realities, humour and translation in an ever-changing mediascape. In M. Dore (ed.) *Humour Translation in the Age of Multimedia* (pp. 116–135). New York: Routledge.
Zaragoza Ninet, G. (2018) Traducción, género y censura: pasado, presente, futuro. In G. Zaragoza Ninet, J.J. Martínez Sierra, B. Cerezo Merchán and M. Richart Marset (coord.). *Traducción, género y censura en la literatura y en los medios de comunicación* (pp. 1–9). Granada: Comares.

Filmography

Abba Live in Concert (1977) Lasse Hallström. Polar Music International & Reg Grundy Productions Pty. Ltd. Australia & Sweden.
Apocalypse Now (1979) Francis Ford Coppola. Zoetrope Studios. USA.
Artist, The (2011) Michel Hazanavicius. La Petite Reine, ARP Sélection, Studio 37, La Class Americane, France 3 Cinema, U Film, Jouror Productions, & JD Prod. France.
Barefoot Contessa, The (1954) Joseph L. Mankiewicz. United Artists. USA.
Blonde Venus (1932) Josef von Sternberg. Paramount Pictures. USA.
Bonnie and Clyde (1967) Arthur Penn. Warner Brothers/Seven Arts & Tatira-Hiller Productions. USA.
Brief Encounter (1945) David Lean. Cineguild. UK.
Calamity Jane (1953) David Butler. Warner Bros. USA.
Deadpool 2 (2018) David Leitch. Kinberg Genre, Maximum Effort, The Donners' Company, TSG Entertainment, & Marvel Entertainment. USA.
Django Unchained (2012) Quentin Tarantino. The Weinstein Company & Columbia Pictures. USA.
Flor de mi secreto, La [Flower of My Secret, The] (1995) Pedro Almodóvar. CiBy 2000 & El Deseo S.A. Spain.
Four Weddings and a Funeral (1994) Mike Newell. PolyGram Filmed Entertainment, Channel Four Films, & Working Title Films. UK.
Full Metal Jacket (1987) Stanley Kubrick. Natant, Stanley Kubrick Productions, & Warner Bros. UK & USA.
Gran Torino (2008) Clint Eastwood. Matten Productions, Double Nickel Entertainment, Gerber Pictures, Malpaso Productions, Media Magik Entertainment, Village Roadshow Pictures, WV Films IV, & Warner Bros. USA.
Greatest Showman, The (2017) Michael Gracey. 20th Century Fox. USA.
Hateful Eight, The (2015) Quentin Tarantino. Double Feature Films, & Film Colony. USA.
Inglourious Basterds (2009) Quentin Tarantino. Universal Pictures, The Weinstein Company, A Band Apart, Zehnte Babelsberg, & Visiona Romantica. USA & Germany.
Joseph and the Amazing Technicolor Dreamcoat (1972) Peter Plummer. Young Vic Company. UK.
Kind Hearts and Coronets (1949) Robert Hamer. Estudios Ealing. UK.
Knives Out (2019) Rian Johnson. FilmNation Entertainment. USA.
Lady Gambles, The (1949) Michael Gordon. Universal International Pictures. USA.
Les Miserables (2012) Tom Hooper. Working Title Films. UK, France & USA.
Lock, Stock and Two Smoking Barrels (1998) Guy Ritchie. Summit Entertainment & HandMade Films. UK.
Lolita (1962) Stanley Kubrick. Seven Arts Productions, A.A. Productions Ltd., Anya Pictures, & Transworld Pictures. UK & USA.

Lolita (1997) Adrian Lyne. Lolita. Pathé. USA.
Mad Max: Fury Road (2015) George Miller. Kennedy Miller Mitchell & Village Roadshow Pictures. Australia.
Moulin Rouge (2001) Baz Luhrmann. Angel Studios Bazmark. USA, Australia & UK.
Nine Perfect Strangers (2021) John-Henry Butterworth, David E. Kelley, & Jonathan Levine. Blossom Films & Made Up Stories. USA.
Once Upon a Time in Hollywood (2019) Quentin Tarantino. Columbia Pictures, Heyday Films, & Polybona Films. USA.
Platoon (1986) Oliver Stone. Hemdale Film & Cinema 86. UK & USA.
Pulp Fiction (1994) Quentin Tarantino. A Band Apart, Jersey Films, & Miramax Films. USA.
Reservoir Dogs (1992) Quentin Tarantino. Live Entertainment & Dog Eat Dog Productions Inc. USA.
Rocknrolla (2008) Guy Ritchie. Warner Bros, Dark Castle Entertainment, Toff Guy Films, & Studio Canal. UK & USA.
Rocky Horror Picture Show, The (1975) Jim Sharman. Twentieth Century Fox Film Corporation. USA & UK.
Roma (2018) Alfonso Cuarón. Participant Media & Esperanto Filmoj. Mexico.
Room at the Top (1959) Jack Clayton. Romulus Films & Remus. UK.
Scarface (1932) Howard Hawks. The Caddo Company. USA.
Snatch (2000) Guy Ritchie. Columbia Pictures Corporation & SKA Films. UK & USA.
Sound of Music, The (1965) Robert Wise. Robert Wise Productions & Argyle Enterprises. USA.
Sweet Girl (2021) Brian Andrew Mendoza. ASAP Entertainment, Pride of Gypsies, & On The Roam. USA.
Tomb Raider (2018) Roar Uthaug. Metro-Goldwyn-Mayer, Warner Bros. Pictures, GK Films, & Square Enix. USA & UK.
Trainspotting (1996) Danny Boyle. Channel Four Films, Figment Films, & The Noel Gay Motion Picture Company. UK.
Trance (2013) Danny Boyle. Pathé, Cloud Eight Films, Decibel Films, & Film4. UK.
Truant Husband, The (1921) Thomas N. Heffron. Rockett Film Corporation. USA.
Ulysses (1967) Joseph Strick. Laser Film Corporation & Ulysses Film Production. UK & USA.
Velvet Buzzsaw (2019) Dan Gilroy. Dease Pictures Inc., & Netflix. USA.

TV Series

Arde Madrid [Burn Madrid] (2018) Paco León & Anna R. Costa. Andy Joke & Movistar+. Spain.
Casa de papel, La [Money Heist] (2017–2021) Álex Pina. Vancouver Media, Atresmedia & Netflix. Spain.
Ellen (1994–1998) Carol Black, Neal Marlens & David S. Rosenthal. Black-Marlens Company & Touchstone Television. USA.
Fleabag (2016–2019) Phoebe Waller-Bridge, Harry Bradbeer & Tim Kirkby. Two Brothers Pictures. UK.
Forbrydelsen [The Killing] (2007–2012) Søren Sveistrup. Danmarks Radio, Norsk Rikskringkasting, Sveriges Television, ZDF Enterprises, Zweites Deutsches Fernsehen, Nordvision, Nordisk Film- & TV-Fond. Denmark, Norway, Sweden & Germany.
Friends (1994–2004) David Crane & Marta Kauffman. Warner Bros. Television and Bright/Kauffman/Crane Productions. USA.
IT Crowd, The (2006–2013) Graham Linehan. Talkback Thames. UK.
Nanny, The (1993–1999) Peter Marc Jacobson & Fran Drescher. Columbia Broadcasting System, Highschool Sweethearts, Sternin and Fraser Ink, & TriStar Television. USA.
Narcos: Mexico (2018–2021) Carlo Bernard & Doug Miro. Mexico.
See (2019–2022) Steven Knight. Chernin Entertainment, & Endeavor Content. Canada.
Sex Education (2019–) Laurie Nunn. Eleven Film. UK.
Squid Game (2021) Hwang Dong-hyuk. Siren Pictures Inc. South Korea.
Succession (2018–) Jesse Armstrong. Gary Sanchez Productions. USA.
White Lotus, The (2021–) Mike White. Rip Cord Productions. USA.

Web Addresses

Web AddressesATRAE (2021) Comunicado sobre la postedición, 13 October 2021. See https://atrae.org/comunicado-sobre-la-posedicion/ (accessed 15 October 2021).

ATRAE (2021) Guía de estilo. Criterios generales para subtitulación y pautado en español. See https://atrae.org/wp-content/uploads/2021/12/Guia-de-estilo-portada-v2.pdf (accessed 15 October 2021).

BBC (2018) Subtitle Guidelines. Version 1.1.8. April 2019. See https://bbc.github.io/subtitle-guidelines/ (accessed 2 September 2021).

Bulthuis, E. (online) Mental illnesses. Terms to use. Terms to avoid. See https://www.healthpartners.com/blog/mental-illnesses-terms-to-use-terms-to-avoid/ (accessed 2 September 2021).

Cadenas, J.F. Netflix vuelve a jugársela con el doble sentido: 'Querrás tragártela enterita'. Newspaper article, 17 January 2020. See https://elpais.com/ccaa/2020/01/17/madrid/1579283472_706278.html (accessed 28 October 2021).

Clark, T. Netflix's 'Money Heist' is the top TV show in the world. Newspaper article, 8 September 2021. See https://www.businessinsider.com/netflixs-money-heist-is-top-tv-show-in-the-world-2021-9 (accessed 10 September 2021).

Kaiman, J. Django Unchained pulled from Chinese cinemas during debut screening. Newspaper article, 11 April 2013. See https://www.theguardian.com/film/2013/apr/11/django-unchained-pulled-chinese-cinemas (accessed 1 September 2021).

Morales, M., Koch, T. and Beauregard, L.P. Netflix removes Castilian Spanish subtitles from Alfonso Cuarón's Roma. Newspaper article, 10 January 2019. See https://english.elpais.com/elpais/2019/01/10/inenglish/1547125380_758985.html (accessed 24 October 2021).

Revoir, P. BBC crackdown subtitles in hit show The Killing after team mistranslates mild Danish expletives into the F-word. Newspaper article, 18 November 2011. See https://www.dailymail.co.uk/tvshowbiz/article-2062937/BBC-crackdown-F-word-subtitles-hit-The-Killing-team-mistranslates-mild-Danish-expletives.html (accessed 10 September 2021).

'What does D/deaf mean?', University of Greenwich. See https://www.gre.ac.uk/study/support/disability/staart/ddeaf (accessed 10 October 2021).

Ye, S. "Trabajo de chinos", "moros en la costa"… las consecuencias del racismo en el lenguaje cotidiano, newspaper article, March 8, 2019. See https://verne.elpais.com/verne/2018/12/02/articulo/1543777568_905717.html (accessed 20 September 2021).

Index

Accessibility 5, 9, 10, 23,
African-American 111
America, American xiii, 30, 31-34, 36, 40, 44, 50, 61, 69, 105, 116,
American English, Am. Eng. 37, 48-51, 54, 59, 62, 65, 109, 111
Audio Description xiii, 5, 10, 23
Audiovisual translation, AVT xi, xiii, 1-6, 8, 11, 14, 19, 21-24, 35, 37, 55-58, 60, 62-64, 84, 86

Bilingual subtitles 14
Blasphemy (blasphemous) 27, 47, 49, 57, 80, 84, 115, 119, 128, 130,
British English, Br. Eng. 50, 51, 54, 65, 109

Calque 1
Compensation 76, 77, 79, 122-124, 128, 129
Culture (cultural) 1, 4-6, 21, 26-31, 36, 37, 44, 46, 51, 52, 54-57, 60, 61, 63, 73-75, 112, 114, 123, 125, 127, 128
Curse (cursing) 34, 47, 54, 59, 115, 121, 138

Dirt(y) 44, 45, 59, 94, 132
Drug(s) 11, 33, 40, 42, 47, 48, 61, 63, 64, 77, 79, 92, 94, 96, 103, 107, 116, 123, 128, 130, 134, 136, 137
Dysphemism 2, 49, 50-52, 59, 64-66, 108-111

English 3, 9-12, 14, 22, 23, 30, 31, 34, 35, 37, 42, 45, 47, 49, 51, 54, 57, 59-64, 67, 71, 73, 82, 84, 86, 102, 103, 113, 120, 122, 123, 127, 131
Euphemism (euphemistic) 2, 30, 44, 48-53, 57, 59-66, 84, 104, 108-113, 118, 125, 130, 132, 135, 138
(Excessive) Alcohol consumption 47, 48, 135
Expletive 30, 46-48, 55, 57, 64, 79, 100, 108, 118, 119, 121, 126, 134
Explicitation 74, 75

Filth(y) 45, 47, 48
Foreign language learning 8, 10, 14
Foul 45, 59, 131

History (historical) 24, 25, 27, 31, 35, 36, 43, 44, 59, 75, 82
Homophobic 53, 61
Hypernym 74, 75
Hyponym 74

Ideological manipulation 1, 2, 26, 31, 61, 82, 84
Impact 2, 20, 26, 32, 45, 51, 54, 55, 57-60, 84, 112, 130
(Im)Politeness 2, 44, 52, 53, 62, 104
Insult 44-49, 52-54, 59-62, 66, 68, 75, 81, 74, 84, 85, 90, 93, 94, 96, 98, 102, 103, 105, 111-116, 118, 120, 123, 125-127, 131-133, 135-141
Interlingual subtitling (subtitles) 6, 8, 13-15
Intralingual subtitling (subtitles) 7-14, 84
Invective 47, 48, 53, 114, 127

Latin America(n) 11, 23, 29, 30, 60, 132
Latin American Spanish 11, 12

Lexical recreation 76, 123, 137, 139
Linguistics (linguistic) 1, 4, 6-9, 13, 15, 17, 19, 20, 23, 30, 32, 38, 46, 51, 52, 55, 57-60, 63, 64, 72, 75, 77, 82, 84, 86, 99, 139
Literal translation 1, 73, 74, 107, 124, 129, 133, 135, 137-140
Load 26, 27, 30, 48-50, 53-56, 58, 60, 62, 63, 78-82, 85-87, 102, 112, 115, 118, 122-140
Loan (loanword) 73, 114

Maintain (maintained, maintaining) 26, 38, 44, 59, 60, 63, 78, 79, 85, 87, 122-141
Manipulation (manipulated) 1, 2, 12, 24-26, 28-31, 37, 61, 63, 82, 84
Multilingual subtitling (subtitles) 6, 14

Neutralise (neutralised, neutralising) 60, 63, 78, 80, 85-87, 122, 124, 126, 127, 129
Non-transfer (not transferred) 78, 80-82, 85-87, 122, 124-127, 129, 133, 136, 138

Offence (offensiveness, offensive) 1-3, 11, 12, 25, 27, 30, 32, 34, 38, 43-60, 62-64, 66, 72-88, 102, 103, 107, 108, 111-140
Omit (omission) 20, 21, 28, 29, 31, 34, 56, 60, 62, 63, 77, 78, 80, 81, 85-87, 100, 103-106, 113, 114, 122, 125, 127, 133, 136, 138
One-liner 16, 18, 38
Orthophemism 2, 49-52, 64-66, 108-111
Orthotypography 19-21

Paralinguistic 1, 9, 13, 15, 57
Patronage 2, 24-26
Pragmatics (pragmatic) 19, 20, 45, 59, 62
Profanity (profane) 32, 34, 47, 49, 59, 119, 126, 127, 136
Proposal 2, 57, 58, 83
Psychology (psychological) 48, 59
Punctuation 20, 21

Racism (racist) 34, 53, 61, 74, 76, 107, 132, 137

Reformulate (reformulation) 73, 78, 101, 102, 106, 107, 123, 125, 126, 128, 130, 132, 134-136, 138-140
Religion (religious) 25, 26, 29, 31, 34, 44-46, 49, 56, 57, 60, 63, 64, 66, 79, 80, 110, 114, 115, 118, 119, 127, 128, 130, 136
Research 1-3, 6, 10, 14, 15, 33, 35, 36, 52, 58-60, 62-64, 72, 81-87
Research design 2, 72, 81, 83, 85-87
Rudeness (rude) 30, 45, 48-52, 55, 73

(Self-)Censorship 1, 2, 24-37, 55, 57, 61, 63, 77, 80, 82, 84, 103, 130
Scatology (scatological) 47, 48, 79, 106, 117, 121, 122, 124, 129, 134
Semiotics (semiotic) 21, 22, 72
Sex (sexual) 28, 29, 31-34, 36, 41, 44, 46, 47, 49-51, 55, 56, 59-63, 65, 66, 75, 94, 97, 106, 109, 111, 112, 116, 119, 120, 129, 132, 135-140
Source language (SL) xiii, 6, 7, 13, 21, 22, 57, 73-76
Source text (ST) xiii, 1, 7, 13, 15, 16, 19-21, 24, 26, 29, 30, 37-42, 52, 56-58, 60, 62, 63, 66-82, 84, 85, 87, 108, 111-140
Slang 4, 11, 30, 34, 43, 44, 50, 59, 104, 105, 112-114, 123, 127, 128, 137
Spain xiii, 1, 2, 4, 9, 10-13, 18, 23-29, 31, 34-37, 46, 53-55, 57, 60, 74-76, 80, 83, 132
Spanish xiii, 1, 3, 10-12, 14-16, 20-25, 27-29, 34-37, 46, 49-51, 53, 54, 57, 59-64, 66, 73, 74-76, 79, 80, 82-84, 86, 87, 99, 100, 102, 103, 105, 107, 111, 118, 119, 121-123, 125, 128, 131, 132, 139
Spatiotemporal restrictions 1, 17, 37, 58, 77, 105, 133
Substitution, substitute 30, 48, 50, 60, 62, 75, 80, 84, 100, 123-125, 128-134, 136-141
Subtitle xiii, 1-27, 29-30, 34, 35, 37, 38, 46, 50, 56-58, 60-64, 66, 72-77, 80, 82-87, 99, 101-107, 111-122, 124-130, 132-141
Subtitler 1, 2, 4, 15-17, 19, 20, 22, 26, 27, 37, 49, 51, 52, 54, 55, 58, 62, 63, 66, 72, 74, 76, 78-81, 85-87, 100-107,

111-115, 118, 119, 122-129, 132-136, 138-141
Subtitling xiii, 1-10, 13-17, 19-21, 23-30, 37, 38, 51, 54-62, 64, 73-78, 81-86, 99, 100, 102, 103, 107, 119, 131, 133, 137, 138
Subtitling conventions 2, 15, 38
Subtitle editors 7, 16, 86
Subtitling for the D/deaf or hard of hearing (SDH) xiii, 5, 9, 10, 13, 15, 23
Swear phrase 116, 119, 127
Swear word 1, 44-48, 52, 55-60, 62, 63, 76, 77, 79, 100, 101, 115, 117, 120, 122-125, 130, 132-134, 138, 140
Swear, swearing 1, 11, 33, 34, 44-49, 51, 52, 54-60, 62, 63, 76, 77, 79, 80, 85, 95, 96, 100, 101, 103, 115-117, 119, 120, 122-125, 127, 130, 132-135, 137, 138, 140
Synchronisation 15, 17, 18

Taboo 1-3, 25, 27, 28, 30, 33, 36, 38, 43-52, 54-64, 66, 72, 73, 76-88, 103, 111, 112, 114, 116-124, 126-130, 132-137, 139, 140
Target language (TL) xiii, 6, 7, 13, 21, 22, 55, 58, 73, 74, 76, 77, 106, 116, 117, 119
Target text (TT) xiii, 1, 7, 8, 15, 19, 21, 27, 30, 38-42, 49, 51, 56, 58, 61-63, 67-82, 84-108, 111-141
Taxonomy 2, 5, 15, 25, 43, 46, 47, 49, 59, 63, 72, 73, 78
Technical constraints 1, 15, 19, 25, 27
Text reduction 2, 15, 19, 25, 38, 99

Threat 28, 42, 47, 49, 52, 71, 90, 107, 121, 127, 133, 136
Transposition 75, 76, 127
Tone up (toned up, toning up) 78, 79, 85, 87, 107, 122, 124-126, 128, 134, 136, 140, 141
Tone down (toned down, toning down) 25, 30, 33, 34, 37, 49, 51, 56, 60, 61, 63, 78-80, 85, 87, 107, 122, 123, 128, 130, 132, 136, 137
Transfer (transferred) 1-4, 6-8, 15, 20, 21, 49, 51, 57, 58, 60, 62, 63, 72, 73, 76-82, 84-87, 102, 104-106, 112, 113, 115-141
Translation method 72, 73
Translation operation 2, 58, 72, 78, 85-87, 122, 128
(Translation) strategy 2, 72, 73, 85, 87-98, 122-140
(Translation) technique 2, 49, 51, 63, 72, 73, 78-82, 85, 87-98, 122-140
Two-liner 16, 18, 38, 57, 100, 107, 108, 112, 113, 116, 118, 120, 121

United Kingdom, UK 2, 9, 13, 23, 24, 33, 34, 36, 42, 54
United States, US 2, 9, 11, 29, 31, 36, 55, 61, 74, 76
Urination (urinate) 47, 48, 51, 65, 109

Violence (violent) 32-34, 47, 49, 113, 117, 121, 125, 136-140
Vulgarity (vulgar) 1, 28, 30, 48, 50, 55, 58, 60, 62, 63, 113, 122, 130, 141

For Product Safety Concerns and Information please contact our EU Authorised Representative:

Easy Access System Europe

Mustamäe tee 50

10621 Tallinn

Estonia

gpsr.requests@easproject.com